D1235881

THE SCAR OF RACE

PAUL M. SNIDERMAN

AND

THOMAS PIAZZA

THE SCAR ᴼꜰ RACE

THE BELKNAP PRESS OF
HARVARD UNIVERSITY PRESS
CAMBRIDGE, MASSACHUSETTS
LONDON, ENGLAND
1993

Book design by Marianne Perlak

Library of Congress Cataloging-in-Publication Data
Sniderman, Paul, M.
The scar of race/Paul M. Sniderman, Thomas Piazza.
p.   cm.
Includes bibliographical references and index.
ISBN 0-674-79010-3 (alk. paper)
1. Race relations.   2. Racism.   I. Piazza, Thomas Leonard.
II. Title.   HT1521.S542 1993   305.8—dc20

93-17063
CIP

To Susan and Mary

ACKNOWLEDGMENTS

A book is like the proverbial message written on a piece of paper, stuck in a bottle, then thrown into the sea. Writing it is an act of faith. Our faith is that, one quarter of a century after the murder of Martin Luther King, Jr., Americans want to know what their fellow citizens think and feel and are prepared to do about the continuing problem of race.

Much has changed in race relations since the passage of the historic civil rights legislation of the 1960s—often without those changes being recognized. To explore the new politics of race in the 1980s and 1990s, we have relied on public opinion surveys—interviews with thousands of ordinary Americans, black and white. Some of the surveys were conducted by other researchers, but our principal sources for the analyses in this book are those surveys we directed ourselves. They use a new approach—experiments embedded in computer-assisted interviews—which allows us to illuminate aspects of Americans' thinking about race hitherto hidden in shadows.

At the head of the list of people to whom we are indebted are the respondents who consented to share their time with us, and to talk—often with striking candor—about the various faces of race in contemporary American politics. The National Science Foundation (through grants SES-8821575 and SES-8508937) supported our field work, while the Survey Research Center at the University of California, Berkeley, under two directors—Percy Tannenbaum and Michael Hout—provided a home for our research project. J. Merrill Shanks, Director of the Computer-Assisted Survey Methods Program, is responsible for development of the full complement of software that makes possible our new approach. The design of the questionnaire used in our California survey was enormously improved thanks to Selma Monsky and Charlotte Coleman. The implementation of that questionnaire on the CASES system for computer-assisted interviewing was carried out by Garry Martin, who also supervised the interviewing. Linda Stork, Carol Royster, and many others were involved in the day-to-day task of collecting the data. The follow-up national survey relied once again on the indispensable contributions of many people at the Survey Research Center. Karen Garrett provided guidance on the design of the questionnaire and on the overall data-collection effort. Yu-Teh Cheng did most of the sampling work, Karen Pladsen set up the questionnaire on the computer, and Charlie Thomas provided programming support. The field work was directed by Janice Clinthorne, with help from Susan Burns, Frank Portman, Tahi Staniford, and Hank Fesler. Bob McCarthy supervised data management and entry of the mailback questionnaire, assisted by Anthony Bowman, Estela de la Cruz, Marykae Josh, and David Seifert. Additional—and invaluable—on-going support was provided by Lisa Kermish, Lani Kask, and Anthony Tyler.

Jonathan Swift remarked that good writing is only a matter of putting the right words in the right places. Many more of the former are in many more of the latter thanks to Susan Wallace, our editor and colleague. Aida Donald's enthusiasm made much easier the daunting task of choosing a congenial home for the book. Indispensable to our getting any words down on paper have been our colleagues at the Survey Research Center: Henry Brady, Neil Fligstein, Fern Glover, Michael Hout, Merrill Shanks, and James Wiley. They have provided a circle of advice and friendship. Making a singular contribution, at every stage, from design through analysis, has been Philip Tetlock.

There would not be a book at all but for our wives, and we dedicate it to them, not as repayment of debt but by way of acknowledgment of our partnership.

Berkeley, California
May 1993

CONTENTS

INTRODUCTION

I still remember—the story coming over the radio—James Meredith was going to enroll, the next day, at the University of Mississippi— the first black ever. A mob of rednecks and drunken students was in the streets, to terrorize one young black, for going to college. We got our sleeping bags, and got in the car. We had at least to witness . . .

Only one memory of only one person, but not unlike many memories of many others. The issue of race was, through and through, a matter of right versus wrong. It was wrong—unequivocally wrong, unambiguously wrong—to make it a crime for a black to drink from the same water fountain as a white, or to play in the same public park, or to attend the same school.

The issue of race, a generation ago, formed the moral highground of American politics. For Americans thoughtful enough to care about moral principle and compassionate enough to care about the worst off, it was a problem of the heart. Today, in the minds of concerned Americans, there is increasingly an intuition—imprecise, tentative, more often implicit than explicit— that the meaning of race as an issue in American life is changing.

The purpose of this book is to examine this intuition—to make it explicit, definite, unequivocal.

Race remains a problem of the heart, but the politics of race has become more complex, more divisive, morally more problematic. What we mean to do, therefore, is to probe how Americans now come to grips with the issues of race. How far is the political thinking of ordinary Americans still driven by prejudice? Is there a new racism more subtle and covert than the old? To what extent is the clash over race still a conflict over whether blacks should be treated as equal to whites? To what extent is it a split over public policies advanced to achieve racial equality? Is racism reinforced by traditional American values such as self-reliance, hard work, individual initiative? What do white Americans think about blacks, and how do these opinions influence their willingness to support social programs that assist blacks? And quite apart from whatever white Americans may say they think about blacks, to what extent are they now willing to treat them as equals, to what extent do they continue to practice racial double standards, one for whites, another—meaner and more censorious—for blacks?

The deepest obstacle to understanding the new politics of race—to recognizing what the conflicts over race are now about—is the universal, if unspoken, assumption that we already understand the place of race in contemporary America. But what we understand is the way the world was a generation ago, a world brilliantly described in the 1940s by Gunnar Myrdal in his classic work *An American Dilemma*. Its message has come to serve as the central, if customarily silent, premise of over a quarter-century of social analysis, public policy, and judicial decision. The dilemma of race, in Myrdal's view, was indeed a "problem in the heart of the American." As he wrote in a much-quoted passage:

> It is there that the interracial tension has its focus. It is there that the decisive struggle goes on. Though our study includes economic, social, and political race relations, at bottom our problem is the moral dilemma of the American—the conflict between the moral valuations on various levels of consciousness and generality. The "American Dilemma" is the ever-raging conflict between, on the one hand, the valuations preserved on the general plane which we shall call the "American Creed," where the American thinks, talks, and acts under the influence of high national and Christian precepts, and, on the

other hand, the valuations on specific planes of individual and group living, where personal and local interests; economic, social, and sexual jealousies; considerations of community prestige and conformity; group prejudice against particular persons or types of people; and all sorts of miscellaneous wants, impulses, and habits dominate his outlook.

For Myrdal, the deepest-lying dynamics of race are not political, economic, social, but moral. Race excites conflict, but conflict of a specific kind: not one American against another American, not even one group of Americans against another group, but each American against himself. On one side of the struggle are liberty, equality, fair play—general valuations "which refer to man as such and not to any particular group or temporary situation"; on the other side are specific valuations "which refer to various smaller groups of mankind or to particular occasions commonly referred to as 'irrational' or 'prejudiced.'" Specific valuations may have the backing of custom or self-interest, but the general valuations have the backing of the American Creed itself. The fundamental principles of the Creed—liberty and equality, the dignity of the individual, the consent of the governed—have become identified with the very idea of America. As Myrdal writes, when the American "worships the Constitution, it is an act of American nationalism, and in this the American Creed is inextricably blended. The liberal Creed, even in its dynamic formulation by Jefferson, is adhered to by every American." Can there be any doubt, then, that in the event of conflict, it is the specific valuations and not the larger Creed that will give way?

Myrdal was alive to the complexity of the conflict between the Creed and race prejudice; indeed, he called attention precisely to the common effort to avoid awareness of conflict between the two, emphasizing that "the whole issue is enveloped in opportune ignorance and unconcernedness on the part of whites." Yet, having acknowledged this, he exploded the idea that white Americans' devotion to the Creed is a matter merely of hypocrisy, that they pay only lip service to the values of liberty and equality, pointing out that

the true hypocrite sins in secret. The American, on the contrary, is strongly and sincerely "against sin," even, and not least, his own sins. He investigates his faults, shouts them from the housetops. If all the world is well informed about the political corruption, organized crime, and faltering system of justice in America, it is primarily not due to its malice but to American publicity about its own imperfections. America's handling of the Negro problem has been criticized most emphatically by white Americans since long before the Revolution, and the criticism has steadily gone on and will not stop until America has completely reformed itself.

For Myrdal, the triumph of the Creed over prejudice was assured over the long run.

Myrdal's conception of an American dilemma brought the politics of race a generation ago into focus, becoming part of the American intellectual heritage. But every inheritance, while conferring a possession, exacts a cost. Most observers today continue to view the problem of race through the lens of Myrdal's argument, seeing the clash over race as a conflict between liberty and equality on the one side and prejudice and self-interest on the other. It remains partly that, but only partly. As we will demonstrate in the chapters that follow, there now is not one issue of race but a number of issues, and the terms of their debate, the swirl of sentiments moving people toward support or opposition, differ significantly from one issue to the next.

In Myrdal's America it was sensible to speak of *the* issue of race. It presented itself, to be sure, in a variety of specific ways. Should blacks be free to compete for the same jobs, on the same terms, as whites? Ought blacks to have the right to live wherever they can afford, just the same as whites? Should black and white children be allowed to go to the same school? But underlying these specific issues, and shaping peoples' reactions to them, was one fundamental question: Should black Americans enjoy the same rights as white Americans, or should they be segregated and oppressed by force of law? In contrast, as we will show, the key to the contemporary politics of race is that there is no longer *one* issue of race but a number of distinct issues, and the politics of these issues differ in telling ways: in the line-up of proponents and opponents; in the forces moving people in one direction or the other; and not least, in the ease or difficulty with which white Americans can be persuaded to change the positions they have taken. A quarter-century ago, what counted was who a policy would benefit, blacks or whites; now, what counts as much, or more, is what the policy aims to accomplish and how it proposes to go about accomplishing it.

To say that racial policies set the terms for arguments over race now is also to say that race *per se* matters less. Prejudice has not disappeared, and in particular circumstances and segments of the society it still has a major impact. But race prejudice no longer organizes and dominates the reactions of whites; it no longer leads large numbers of them to oppose public policies to assist blacks across-the-board. It is, as we shall show, simply wrong to suppose that the primary factor driving the contemporary arguments over the politics of race is white racism.

In saying this, we are not at all crossing swords with thoughtful observers who hear the suspicion, anger, and resentment on all sides of the racial divide nowadays. On the contrary, we shall make a considerable effort to establish the continuing prevalence of stigmatizing images of blacks. For example, strikingly large numbers of whites—and blacks—perceive blacks to be failing to make a genuine effort to deal with their problems, and they are perfectly willing to say it publicly. But the arguments over race now cut at new angles. To treat the politics of race as though it is only about race and not about politics misrepresents the nature of contemporary disagreements over issues of race. This study accordingly represents an effort, above all, to make clear *what* Americans are disagreeing over now—not a generation ago—and *why*.

As a point of departure, in Chapter 1 we will emphasize the new patterns of conflict over race. A generation ago, one basic line of division ran through the American public, separating opponents and proponents of public policies intended to assist blacks— regardless of what the particular policies aimed to accomplish or how they proposed to accomplish it. Now, different lines of cleavage run across different issues. Arguments over government spending are not the same as arguments over affirmative action, and neither are interchangeable with arguments over fair housing. Yet the language in which we talk about race has remained the same. And just because the words and habits of thought are so familiar, we fail to recognize we are intermixing different problems, confusing different arguments, in the end leading more than a few to conclude that disagreements over race represent not principled differences but bad faith.

No aspect of the problem of race in American life is more often discussed, or less well understood, than the standing of blacks in the popular culture. It has become nearly a cliché to talk about how white racism is now subtle, and how whites are now reluctant to publicly express negative views of blacks, all by way of trying to establish that a problem of racism still persists; it has just gone underground. But if you want to understand how whites feel about blacks, you must listen to what they actually say. Having done so, we shall demonstrate in Chapter 2 that, contrary to fashionable opinion, whites are not reticent about commenting negatively about blacks. Large numbers of them—on occasion a majority even in an especially affluent and uncommonly liberal part of the country—will express frankly negative evaluations of blacks, even to a total stranger.

What is behind this? Some contemporary observers have broken away from the liberal consensus that has shaped the discussion of race since Myrdal. Turning him on his head, they contend that a new racism has entered mainstream America, a racism whose wellsprings are the very values on which Americans pride themselves: hard work, individual initiative, self-reliance—in a word, individualism. Much scholarly effort has gone into this work on the new racism, and still more concern for the well-being of blacks, but as we shall show in Chapter 2, the view that mainstream American values foster racism confuses two kinds of traditional values. The traditional American value of individualism does not foster either antipathy to blacks or opposition to public policies intended to help them; on the other hand, traditional authoritarian values like obedience and conformity promote both.

To talk candidly about the problem of prejudice has become difficult. For both straightforward and subtle reasons, many feel the need to insist that the contemporary conflict over racial policies is still being driven by bigotry, both openly expressed and covert; that white racism remains a dominating force in our culture; that opposition to any policy intended to assist blacks is, in itself, proof of race prejudice. All this is wrong; and we shall demonstrate it to be wrong. It has, however, had a corrupting effect. On the one hand, the attribution of the term "racist" has become indiscriminate. At public meetings, it has become routine for opponents to silence those questioning a racial policy—for example, speech codes at universities or hearings on minority set-asides in municipal contracts—by labeling them racist. For that matter, it is not uncommon even for scholars to charge, in a blanket indictment, that opposition to affirmative action is, in and of itself, proof of bigotry. The demagogic use of the charge of prejudice has done much to poison the contemporary discussion of race, persuading many scholars as well as citizens that the concept of prejudice has lost any serious meaning and become no more than a term of political abuse.

One of our primary objectives, accordingly, is to demonstrate that prejudice still matters politically. Because the use of the term has become so politicized, we have made a special effort to demonstrate that prejudice, in the straightforward sense of outright antipathy to those who are different by virtue of the color of their skin or their religious orientation, remains with us. Indeed, one of the best ways to tell how whites feel about blacks, as we shall demonstrate in Chapter 2, is to find out how they feel about Jews. Unreasoning aversion to others merely on the ground of a difference in their appearance or religion *does* carry through to people's political views, significantly influencing the positions they take on issues of race.

This study documents—for the first time—not just how white Americans feel about black Americans, but the extent to which whites continue to practice a racial double standard against blacks. Our "laid-off worker" experiment and "equal opportunity" experiment, both described in Chapter 3, help us to identify when racial double standards manifest themselves and, as important, when they don't. But the larger theme uncovered by these two experiments is the positive role of education. Many critics have charged that schooling does not genuinely encourage racial tolerance and open-mindedness; it merely teaches people the right thing to say. Our findings in Chapter 3 will show that this cynicism about education is wrong. Education is the institution of contemporary American society that fights the actual practice of racial double standards more effectively than any other.

The contemporary discussion of race confuses what white Americans think about blacks with what they think about public policies dealing with blacks. The two are not the same. It would be comforting to think that the clash over the place of race in American public life would disappear if only bigotry could be overcome. But the problem is more complex. For example, prejudice is one cause of the perception of blacks as more violent than whites. But it is far from true that every person who perceives blacks as more violent is a bigot. On the contrary, many people—including many blacks—do so because it fits their personal experience or their impressions picked up through the the mass media. And, ironically, negative racial stereotypes would matter less politically if they were only an expression of prejudice. For, as we shall show in Chapter 4, a judgment that blacks are not making a genuine effort to cope with their problems has as heavy an impact on the political thinking of a person who is *not* prejudiced as it does on the thinking of one who *is*.

To focus only on racism in offering an account of the politics of race omits politics itself. People's reactions to a particular policy are presumed to be a product of social and economic factors—how they make their living, when and where they were raised and hence how they were socialized, how they feel about blacks— indeed, nearly every factor *except the policy itself*. But to give an account of people's reactions without taking into account what they are reacting *to* is misleading in a fundamental way. The presumption that whites' objections to racial quotas or preferential treatment as unfair is a smokescreen, intended to disguise either their racism or their fear that they will lose the privileges they illegitimately enjoy because of the racism of others, has led many observers to read the politics of affirmative action exactly the wrong way around. Certainly some whites dislike affirmative action because they dislike blacks (a racial bigot is not going to be a champion of racial quotas in behalf of blacks). But, as our "mere mention" experiment in Chapter 4 will show, it is unfortunately also true that a number of whites dislike the idea of affirmative action so much and perceive it to be so unfair that they have come to dislike blacks as a consequence. Hence the special irony of the contemporary politics of race. In the very effort to make things better, we have made some things worse. Strong arguments can be made in behalf of affirmative action, but its political price must also be recognized. Wishing to close the racial divide in America, we have widened it.

But to reduce the contemporary politics of race to affirmative action would be as serious a mistake as reducing it to racism. The most important feature of race as an issue in American public life today, we want to urge, is the diversity it manifests at every level. The most straightforward, yet curiously the most neglected, example of the diversity of contemporary racial politics is the strikingly different levels of public support different racial policies enjoy. Some policies—like affirmative action or busing—are supported by only a small fraction of the public, often on the order of only one in five or fewer. Other racial policies—like direct government assistance or antidiscrimination laws—command the support of a majority of whites. Moreover, not only do different racial policies enjoy different levels of public support, but also the factors underlying whites' racial policy positions differ in significant ways from one type of racial policy to another, as we shall discuss in Chapter 5. A swirl of forces—political ideology, prejudice, ideas of fairness and effort—are at work to shape the public's reactions to specific racial policies, and their relative importance varies twice over. It varies, first, from one racial issue to another, and second, even for the very same issue, from one part of American society to another.

The contemporary politics of race is complex, but it is not chaotic. It has a form, albeit a complex form. Every racial issue is not different from every other; rather, specific issues of race take on their defining characteristics depending on the larger policy agenda to which they belong.

We shall focus on three of these policy agendas: the social welfare agenda, which centers on the provision of income, services, and training to improve the economic and social circumstances of blacks; the equal treatment agenda, which centers on banning deliberate discrimination based on race; and the race-conscious agenda, which centers on awarding preferential treatment to blacks to compensate for past discrimination. Their politics are not completely divorced. There are common elements, due partly to the thin slice of the white public still obdurately opposed to any effort to assist blacks, due still more significantly to the thicker slice ready to back a range of racial policies to make things go better for blacks. Yet, the fundamental point is that the politics of social welfare is not the same as the politics of affirmative action, and the politics of fair housing differs from both.

The politics of the three racial agendas differ in levels of popular support, in the line-up of proponents and opponents, and in the configuration of social and economic forces that incline ordinary Americans to take one or the other side of a specific racial issue. And for that very reason, the politics of the three agendas differ in yet another and politically still more consequential way—namely, in the willingness of people to change their minds about a given issue.

The fact that the positions whites take on racial issues are pliable—that large numbers of them may be readily induced to change their stand given only a relatively slight pressure to do so—has gone virtually unsuspected. It has been taken for granted that however hazy ordinary citizens' views are on many issues of the day, when it comes to race they know which side of the fence they're on—and, apart from those affecting a concern they do not genuinely feel for the welfare of blacks, that is where they are going to stay. It has simply been assumed that on issues of race the positions of white Americans are fixed.

This unspoken—and, as we shall show in Chapter 6, quite erroneous—assumption of fixity has hidden a vital feature of the contemporary politics of race. Believing that whites are more or less wedded to their positions on issues of race, political and civic leaders have concluded there is very little room for maneuver—or, indeed, very little point to it. Why calculate whether one's appeal and tactics on an issue will be persuasive if whites' minds are closed to any appeal to rethink their views on race?

Americans *are* dug in on some issues of race, affirmative action being a paradigmatic example. But the common impression of the American public as divided into two more or less fixed armies clashing over race is fundamentally mistaken. On many issues, whites are not stuck in place. They are open to arguments against their point of view. Their positions are subject to change.

Their willingness to change has limits, but the potential for change in racial politics has gone virtually unsuspected—and certainly unstudied. Accordingly, in our "counter-arguments" experiment in Chapter 6 we shall focus on a set of pivotal questions: How hard is it to talk whites out of the positions they take on racial issues? Is it easier to talk them out of their views on some kinds of racial issues, harder to dislodge them from their positions on others? Is it easier to talk people on one side of a racial issue out of their position than people on the other side out of theirs, easier to induce proponents of government assistance for blacks to qualify or give up their position in the course of argument than to induce opponents of government activism to yield theirs? Putting aside the details of the answers we shall spell out later, we want to underline here a fundamental sense in which there is a *politics* of race. Politics centers on the continuing struggle to create new majorities, or to hold on to old ones, and over the largest number of issues of race, the outcome is up for grabs. There may be little room for movement on an issue like affirmative action, but substantial room for argument and counter-argument can be found around most other racial issues. The majorities of the moment are not one-sided, and the number of people whose preferences are pliable is sizeable. Indeed, if one lesson from our findings deserves more emphasis than any other, it is this: although the fact and shame of racial inequality is irremediably part of our past, what can and will be done about the continuing problem of race is not foreordained. It depends instead on how both political leaders and the larger public combine to make collective choices: it depends, that is to say, on politics. Each side can attract significantly more citizens to its cause. Or—by its political tactics and symbolic assertions—repel them.

This study presents the results of a number of large-scale surveys of the American public—five in all, three national and two regional—and has involved analysis of a still larger number. Of the five, we shall pay the most attention to one, which introduces a radically new way of conducting studies of public opinion. By taking advantage of the power of computers to carry out interviews of an order of complexity and variability not previously possible, we can expose aspects of the thinking of Americans about race always before in the shadows. Combining the advantages of experimental design and the standard representative sample allows us to document for the first time in a public opinion survey the practice of racial double standards—the readiness to deny blacks exactly the same benefit that would be awarded whites—and demonstrate where in American society it is most and least prevalent. Also, we can demonstrate, again for the first time, how the mere mention of affirmative action increases negative reactions to blacks. And, not least, we can capture for the first time the pliability of racial policy preferences, by making the public opinion interview more nearly resemble ordinary conversation, with the push and pull of argument and counter-argument.

Our findings point in more than one direction. Some of our results give grounds for optimism, some for pessimism, and some can be read either way. But our results are not of a piece because life is not of a piece, and so we shall argue above all for the need to think anew about the problem of race in American life, to see it as it is now and not as it was a generation ago, to recognize and to respect its complexities and ironies.

Mindful of this, we want to set out, as clearly and distinctly as we can, the principal findings of our study:

- It is no longer appropriate to speak of *the* issue of race. There are a variety of clashes, driven by different ideals, fears, and expectations of gain and loss. The politics of affirmative action is not the same as the politics of government spending, and both differ from the politics of fair housing.

- Notwithstanding the cliché that whites will not openly endorse negative racial stereotypes for fear of appearing to be racist, large numbers of them—rarely less than one in every five and sometimes as many as one out of every two—agree with frankly negative characterizations of blacks, particularly characterizations of blacks as irresponsible and as failing to work hard and to make a genuine effort to deal with their problems on their own.

- Racism—whether defined in terms of negative characterizations of blacks, of opposition to policies to assist blacks, or of the practice of racial double standards in judgments of who is entitled to government assistance—is not built-in to core American values. Contrary to recent claims that racism is now stimulated by traditional American values, a quite different set of values is at work—not individualist but authoritarian.

- Liberals are more likely to favor, and conservatives more likely to oppose, the use of government to redress racial inequalities. But contrary to assertions that conservatives' opposition to government spending on behalf of blacks is a form of racism, taking advantage of the power of genuine experimental randomization, we found that ideological differences over racial public policies represent genuine differences of political outlook rather than covert racism.

- Claims for government assistance made on behalf of blacks as *individuals* are treated as fairly as those made on behalf of individual whites, and indeed, insofar as race makes a difference, a black who has lost his or her job meets with a more sympathetic and generous response than a white who has lost his or her job. On the other hand, when it comes to judgments about what blacks as a group are entitled to, a racial double standard manifestly persists.

- Contrary to the common suggestion that formal schooling teaches people primarily the socially desirable thing to say, education is the institution in contemporary American society that contributes most powerfully to establishing genuine racial tolerance, and its contribution not only shapes how whites feel toward blacks but their willingness to treat them the same as whites.

- Prejudice no longer dominates the reactions of white Americans, leading them to reject across-the-board public policies designed to assist blacks. Prejudice still helps sustain negative characterizations of blacks, but, paradoxically, its impact on the political thinking of whites is strongest where it has been least remarked (on issues of social welfare) and weakest where it has been most emphasized (on questions of affirmative action).

- The conflict over the new race-conscious agenda has given an impression of progress, suggesting forward movement from earlier and morally less controversial racial issues of the 1950s. Ironically, however, the new disagreements have obscured the persistence of many of the old ones, with Americans still deeply divided over the use of government even to ensure equal treatment for blacks.

- Finally, and perhaps most importantly, the positions that whites take on issues of race are pliable to a degree never suspected. Substantial numbers—on some issues as many as four in every ten—can be talked out of the position they have taken by relatively weak counter-arguments, affirmative action not surprisingly being a major exception. And since preferences are pliable on both sides of racial issues, majorities can be assembled either in favor of or in opposition to many public policies aimed to assist blacks. Our future is not fixed by our past.

1

THE VARIETY OF
RACIAL POLITICS

Ordinary citizens are not in the habit of paying close attention to public affairs even at those moments when they are paying their closest attention, as in the course of a presidential election. One consequence is that an impressively large number of citizens know embarrassingly little about public affairs. Two out of every three citizens, for example, are ignorant of the term of office for United States senators. For that matter, one out of every two does not know which party controls Congress. And however large the holes in their knowledge of domestic affairs, the gaps yawn still larger when it comes to foreign policy. For example, nearly 40 percent of one survey sample believed that Israel is an Arab nation. Such ignorance seems to be an enduring feature of mass politics. Comparisons of citizens' knowledge of politics over the last three decades, optimistically interpreted, suggest that increases in awareness have been modest; pessimistically interpreted, they hint that the prevailing level of awareness about politics and public affairs has actually declined if we take account of the improved educational opportunities over the last three decades.

The fitfulness of the public's attention to politics exacts a price not simply in the decreased probability that citizens will have informed opinions about issues of the day but also in the decreased likelihood that they will put their various opinions together coherently. Overarching political orientations such as liberalism and conservatism do not play a central role in organizing and disciplining the political thinking of the average citizen. The bulk of voters who claim to be of, say, a liberal persuasion do not reliably line up in support of specific liberal policy initiatives, with the bulk of conservatives arrayed against them. Across a wide swathe of issues, so far from organizing their ideas neatly and consistently, ordinary citizens tend to arrange them more higgledy-piggledy.

But not when it comes to race. Race, according to the classic studies of public opinion in the 1960s, is the great exception to the rule that public affairs fall at the periphery of ordinary citizens' interests. We want, therefore, in the next section to sketch the consensus view of how white Americans think about issues of race. Then in the rest of the chapter we will present evidence to suggest that the consensus view no longer applies.

THE CONSENSUS VIEW

The classic studies of race and public opinion agree that whites respond to the problem of race as they do to no other issue on the public agenda. They may care little about many issues of the day; they may have thought little about them; and the opinions they express about them may be superficial, no more than an impulse of the moment. But all of this is very different when it comes to race. The feelings of ordinary Americans on questions of race run strong. The issue of race matters deeply to them, and they know where they stand on it. Race is a red-flag issue, and even if their interest in public affairs is minimal and sporadic, even if they find discussions of issues of the day arid and boring, the issue of race hits home, and their response to it is immediate, emotional, visceral.

In the parlance, race is an "easy issue." Some issues demand substantial amounts of knowledge to work through; in contrast, whites can be nearly completely ignorant of the provenance or details of a policy like busing and all the same know, almost instantly, just where they stand on it. Race is a symbolic issue, and when they take sides on an issue like busing, it is the symbols of race—the mental picture of black and white together—not the specific and technical details of scheduling and classroom size to which they are reacting. In deciding whether to support or oppose integration or more government assistance to improve the living conditions of blacks, the ordinary American does not carefully work through a calculus of costs and benefits, or scrutinize whether the means proposed are efficient and appropriate to the ends sought. Rather, the ends themselves—the willingness to accept blacks as equals and the readiness to sacrifice in order to achieve racial equality—dictate their answers.

According to the consensus view, the clash over race in American public life, at its heart, is driven by an argument between conflicting visions of what America should be like, not by simple disagreement over how most efficiently to achieve a consensual goal. Moreover, while other issues come and go, race has endured on the American agenda. It was a bitter and divisive issue when every American who is now an adult was a child, and it threatens to be so when every one of their children has finally become an adult. And the sheer length of time that race has stood out in American life has bred a bone-deep familiarity with it, an immediate and sure sense on the part even of citizens ordinarily uninterested in public affairs that they know exactly where they stand on the matter of race.

The character of race as an issue—the fact that it has so strong a hold on whites' deepest antipathies and fears—has defined the fundamental structure of conflict over race. Loose, shifting, amorphous coalitions are the rule for the ordinary run of issues. In contrast, the structure of conflict over racial policies is simple and deep. Conflict over issues of race is cumulative. Whites who oppose racial integration in education tend also to oppose more government assistance to improve employment opportunities for blacks—and busing, and fair housing, and so on over the array of racial policies. Indeed, whites' responses to specific issues of race—to busing, to housing, to employment, to education—are so consistent that it is plain these particular issues do not have an independent identity; they are merely specific illustrations of a larger and deeper division over race itself.

Race is an emotional issue, a "gut" issue, an issue on which whites know how they feel even if their knowledge of the details of any particular policy dealing with race—whether busing or government assistance in housing or educational enhancement—is altogether sketchy. And precisely because race is a gut issue, opposition to racial equality does not take the form of an ordinary coalition—loose, temporary, inconsistent. Instead, it is spearheaded by a formidable, enduring bloc that offers consistent and tenacious opposition to any effort to make things better for blacks, on issue after issue.

This image of racial politics as being fought across-the-board, the same bloc of citizens arrayed in opposition issue after issue, captures the core of racial politics measured in the classic studies of race and American public opinion. The image, it should be underlined, is not meant merely metaphorically: the notion is not simply that ordinary citizens are likely to oppose, say, more government spending in behalf of blacks if they oppose busing. Rather, the response of whites to specific issues of race, it is said, is so massively consistent that plainly the particulars of specific issues and policies are not, in themselves, important. What matters is whether a policy is meant to make things better or worse for blacks; and the simple, overall intent of policies is decisive because the reactions of whites to racial issues rest not on judgments about particular policies but instead on their deeper feelings toward blacks. The more they dislike blacks, the more likely they are to dislike a policy designed to help blacks—whatever its specific objectives or the particular means by which it proposes to accomplish these goals. At a fundamental level, then, the politics of any given racial issue is essentially the same as the politics of any other. Because race is an emotional issue at its core, as Philip Converse in his seminal study of public opinion pointed out, the whole gamut of racial policies tends "to boil down to the same single question: Are you sympathetic to Negroes as a group, are you indifferent to them, or do you dislike them?"

The dominating feature of racial politics is thus consistency, but not because people decide to pay special attention to political issues that concern blacks and to scrutinize minutely all proposals for public action having to do with race. Rather, according to the consensus view, the politics of race has coherence precisely because it doesn't have content. Political ideas of any size, whether large (in the form of an ideology, for example, conservatism) or small (in the form of an objection, for example, to increasing the deficit) do not enter in any substantial way into this account of citizens' thinking about the politics of race. Paradoxically, then, ordinary citizens can be consistent precisely because they are not being distracted by any of the actual features of the proposals for public action concerning blacks that are set before them. It is of little importance if the effort to fight discrimination is to be carried out by the federal government or state and local government; of little importance if the purpose of a policy is to provide poor blacks with some access to medical care or to assure them of their right to vote. What matters—and for all practical purposes, all that matters—is how they feel about blacks.

The consensus view of racial issues as sketched here has support from survey results obtained a generation ago. The consistency of citizens' reactions to different issues can be measured in terms of a correlation coefficient: the bigger the size of the coefficient, the more consistent their responses. If their positions are perfectly consistent, the correlation coefficient will be 1.0. If they are not at all consistent, the correlation coefficient will be .0. For issues of race, as Carmines and Stimson have reported, the average correlation for the period 1956–1960 was .54; in contrast, for nonracial issues the average correlation was .15. This result, for those familiar with the arithmetic of public opinion statistics, has always been taken as a hat-doffing demonstration that racial policies, in the minds of ordinary Americans, fundamentally "boil down to the same single question: Are you sympathetic to Negroes as a group, are you indifferent to them, or do you dislike them?"

ISSUE PLURALISM

This picture of the politics of race in the 1950s and 60s was so convincingly drawn in a series of classic studies of the period that its continuing verisimilitude has been unquestioningly accepted. But a generation has passed. Much has changed in many spheres of life, race among them. It is time to look again at how Americans think about issues of race. Are their reactions still dominated by their gut feelings toward blacks? Do they respond to policies—for example, affirmative action and set-asides—that no one had dreamt of thirty years ago in the same terms as they react to more conventional forms of government assistance?

We shall show that the character of racial politics has changed. There is no longer a single, overarching issue but a variety of issues on the table, and their politics are distinct. We are not suggesting that different racial policies have nothing in common— that the ordinary citizen believes that a proposal to increase the amount of government spending in behalf of blacks has no connection whatever with a proposal to improve blacks' access to quality education or medical care. But a distinguishing mark of the contemporary politics of race is the number of fundamentally different arguments being conducted over race at the same time. The clash over affirmative action is not the same as the conflict over more conventional forms of government assistance, and differences of opinion over an issue like fair housing have their own dynamic.

This diversity of responses to racial issues is, we want to suggest, the single most important feature of contemporary racial politics; and to document it we shall bring to bear three studies: the two largest, regularly conducted academic surveys of American public opinion—the National Election Study and the General Social Survey—plus the special survey we ourselves conducted in the San Francisco-Oakland Bay Area. The key question we want to address in all three studies is whether whites' responses to issues of race can still be reduced to how they feel about blacks. The crucial piece of information needed to answer this question is the consistency of whites' reactions to different racial policies. The more consistent their reactions to racial issues, the more those issues boil down to the same single question; the less consistent their responses, the more they tend to react to particular racial policies in their own terms.

Let us begin with the National Election Study (NES). The 1986 NES canvassed reactions to a set of racial issues, including: Should federal spending to assist blacks be increased or decreased? Should the government in Washington make every effort to improve the social and economic position of blacks, or should it not make any special effort to assist blacks because they should help themselves? Should blacks be given preference in hiring and promotion because of past discrimination, or is it wrong to do so because it discriminates against whites? And should openings in college admission be reserved for black students because of past discrimination, or would racial quotas discriminate against whites? The table on page 22 shows the extent to which whites react consistently to this set of racial issues, measuring the consistency of reactions to racial issues with correlation coefficients. For variables of this type, a correlation of about .30 is reasonably large.

As the table shows, these four racial issues do not belong to one homogeneous bloc but instead form two distinct clusters—or, as we shall call them, policy agendas. One policy agenda centers on conventional proposals for government activism in behalf of the disadvantaged. Thus, citizens treat a proposal to increase federal spending to assist blacks as raising essentially the same issue as a proposal that the government in Washington improve the social and economic position of blacks. If they support one, they are highly likely to support the other; if they oppose one, they are highly likely to oppose the other. And it is surely obvious why reactions to this pair of proposals should be so consistent. It is not simply that both concern blacks; equally important, both center on the question of how active an effort the federal government should make in ameliorating social and economic disadvantages. Both policies are thus central to a larger argument that has been carried on in American politics since at least the Great Depression, an argument which, though made in behalf of different groups from time to time, has hinged on an abiding conflict over the proper role of government, and particularly the federal government, in seeing to the social welfare of citizens. We shall therefore refer to policies of this stripe as belonging to a *social welfare agenda*.

A second, and quite distinct, policy agenda can be seen in the case of affirmative action. People who take the position that blacks should be given preference in hiring and promotion are highly likely to take the position that racial quotas should be imposed in college admissions; conversely, those who oppose racial quotas in schools are highly likely to oppose preferential hiring and promotion at work. There is, of course, nothing surprising in this; it would be remarkable if a person supported racial quotas in hiring for jobs but opposed them in admitting students to colleges. But

Consistency of whites' positions on racial policies: National Election Study			
Racial policy	More government spending for blacks	Improve socioeconomic position of blacks	Affirmative action – jobs
Improve socioeconomic position of blacks	.39	**Correlations between policies**	
Affirmative action – jobs	.25	.22	
Affirmative action – college	.25	.24	.43

Source: 1986 National Election Study, Form A. Minimum N=710.
Note: The correlation coefficients reported here and in all subsequent tables, charts, and figures are Pearson product moment correlation coefficients. The full text of questions used in tables, charts, and figures can be found in the back of this book.

the reason that this result appears to be only common sense is precisely because most of us know from personal experience that, in discussion nowadays of racial issues, disagreements over affirmative action have their own character and tone; and to mark this distinctiveness, we shall refer to proposals to establish racial quotas or to practice preferential treatment in behalf of blacks, whatever particular domain they are applied to, as exemplifying a *race-conscious policy agenda.*

Our results vividly underline the distinctiveness of these two approaches—the social welfare agenda and the race-conscious agenda—to the problem of race. Notwithstanding a modest tendency to consistency across racial policies all in all, responses are far more consistent to issues from a common agenda, whether it is the social welfare or the race-conscious agenda, than to policies from different agendas—so much so that correlation coefficients measuring consistency within agendas are almost twice the size of coefficients between policies in different agendas.

This pattern of results, moreover, indicates that the common suggestion that affirmative action has become a litmus test revealing whites' "true" feelings toward blacks is plainly wrong. If you want to predict whether a person will support more vigorous government efforts to improve the social and economic position of blacks, you are far better off finding out their response to increasing federal spending for blacks than to imposing racial quotas in school admissions. Beyond this, if the results we have seen are dependable, there has been a sea change in the temper of racial politics. Whereas all public policies designed to assist blacks used to evoke the same reaction from whites, today, social welfare policies and race-conscious policies are evaluated in distinguishably different terms.

The 1986 General Social Survey (GSS) broadens considerably the coverage of particular racial issues and, no less usefully, varies somewhat the specific terms in which particular racial policies are formulated. Six issues have been selected for examination: Whether we are spending too much money on improving the condition of blacks, or spending too little, or spending about the right amount? Whether the government has a special obligation to help improve the living standards of blacks because they have been discriminated against for so long or, alternatively, whether the government should not be giving special treatment to blacks? Whether black and white school children should be bused from one district to another? Whether a homeowner should be able to decide for himself whom to sell his house to, even if he prefers not to sell to blacks, or whether it should be illegal for homeowners to refuse to sell to someone because of race or color? Whether, if their party nominated a black for president, they would vote for him if he were qualified for the job? And finally, whether they would have any objections to sending their children to a school where half of the children are black?

Looking at the table on page 24, one can immediately see a pair of racial issues—whether government has a special obligation to help improve the living standards of blacks and whether government spending to improve conditions for blacks should be increased—that have much in common. Whites who favor spending more government money in behalf of blacks, it is a good

Racial policy	More government spending for blacks	Obligation to help	Busing	Fair housing	Black president
Consistency of whites' positions on racial policies: General Social Survey					
Obligation to help	.33	Correlations between policies			
Busing	.12	.19			
Fair housing	.17	.15	.20		
Black president	.18	.15	.07	.22	
Integrate your child	.18	.12	.11	.18	.30

Source: 1986 General Social Survey. Minimum N=525.

bet, also believe that the government has a special obligation to help improve the living conditions of blacks because they have been discriminated against for so long; conversely, those who believe the government is already spending too much money in behalf of blacks are an excellent bet to believe that the government does not have an obligation to help improve the living conditions of blacks. This result from the General Social Survey virtually duplicates a finding from the National Election Study, and surely it is perfectly obvious why. These particular policies are really just specific illustrations of a larger theme drawn from the persisting clash over the merits of a more liberal, New Deal style of government as against a more conservative emphasis on the limits of government and the need for fiscal restraint—an argument which, far from being confined to blacks, has been a classic motif of American politics since Franklin Delano Roosevelt.

In addition, a second cluster appears. A willingness of whites to support school integration goes hand-in-hand with a willingness to vote for a black (who is otherwise qualified) for president. The pair thus captures something of whites' willingness to treat blacks as equals, and what is worth reflection is the fact that this willingness, though positively correlated with a readiness to support social welfare assistance for blacks, is only modestly so.

Both the General Social Survey and the National Election Study, then, point to a distinctive cluster of racial policies—or, in our terms, a policy agenda—organized around the larger issue of governmental responsibility for social welfare needs. Beyond this, the GSS results make explicit another aspect of contemporary thinking about issues of race. Simply put, a large number of racial issues stand substantially on their own. Busing, for example, has little to do with government spending for blacks. The issue of whether government should make an extra effort to improve the living conditions of blacks has little to do with the question of whether a homeowner should be allowed to refuse to sell his house to buyers because of race or color. And reactions to a black running for president have little to do with reactions to the busing of black and white school children from one district to another—or to the amount the government ought to spend to help blacks, or to the issue of fair housing, or to the desirability of school integration. We do want to point out that there are no issues on which people systematically shift sides—no occasions, that is, when the bulk of the people who favor one policy to assist blacks change in unison to oppose another policy to help them, and vice versa. But having said this, we must emphasize the clear lesson to be drawn from these findings: so far from white Americans responding to the contemporary array of racial issues *en bloc*, either opposing or favoring them across-the-board, the consistency of their responses to many racial issues is now conspicuous for its modesty.

The third study we shall examine, the Race and Politics (RAP) Survey, also conducted in 1986, was explicitly designed to incorporate the strengths both of the National Election Study and the General Social Survey, in addition to introducing the new computer-assisted methods which are its unique contribution. The coverage of racial issues in the Race and Politics Survey is thus more extensive and more varied than in either the NES or the GSS, and includes: Whether the government ought to see to it that blacks get fair treatment in jobs or whether this is not the government's business and it should stay out of it. Whether the government in Washington should increase spending for programs to help blacks or whether blacks should rely only on themselves. Whether homeowners should be able to decide for themselves whom to sell their houses to, even if they prefer not to sell to blacks, or whether homeowners should not be allowed to refuse to sell to someone because of race or color. Whether or not there should be a law to ensure that a certain number of federal contracts go to minority contractors. Whether, because of past discrimination, colleges and universities should reserve openings for black students who don't meet the usual standards or whether there should be no such quotas. And whether or not school children should be bused to schools out of their own neighborhoods to achieve racial integration.

Which of these issues share large elements in common? Which tend to be free-standing, with people evaluating them in their own terms? Looking at the table on page 27, one can see the same cleavage over the social welfare agenda we saw in the first two studies. The proposals to increase government spending to assist blacks and to have the government ensure fair treatment in jobs are both classic expressions of government activism in behalf of the disadvantaged; and the reactions of citizens to them are appropriately and strikingly consistent. The person who believes that the government ought to stay out of overseeing hiring is highly likely also to believe that it is up to blacks to take care of their own problems; and conversely, the person who favors more government spending in behalf of blacks is highly likely also to believe that the government ought to see to it that they get fair treatment in jobs. Again, both policies are part of the larger political controversy over the desirability of government activism in meeting social welfare needs of citizens—a controversy which has been at the center of contention in American politics for half a century.

These two policies to one side, however, the remainder of racial policies have remarkably little in common. The issue of fair housing is a particularly striking example of the extent to which

Racial policy	Ensure fair job treatment	More government spending for blacks	Fair housing laws	Affirmative action – college	Minority set-asides
Consistency of whites' positions on racial policies: Race and Politics Survey					
More government spending for blacks	.46	Correlations between policies			
Fair housing laws	.27	.22			
Affirmative action – college	.16	.27	.14		
Minority set-asides	.22	.27	.09	.23	
Busing	.20	.21	.17	.21	.23

Source: 1986 Race and Politics Survey. Minimum N=730.

specific issues of race tend to stand or fall largely on their own terms. People who think that racial discrimination in the sale of housing should be illegal are only slightly—ever so slightly—more likely than those who think the opposite to believe that a certain number of federal contracts should go to minority contractors. And although statistically discernible, the linkages between fair housing and affirmative action, or fair housing and busing, stand out not for the magnitude but for the modesty of the connections between them.

Fair housing does seem to stand more on its own than most other contemporary issues, but it only illustrates in a more vivid way the distinctive feature of the contemporary politics of race. As compared with the clash over race in the 1950s and 60s, when specific issues were merged into the fundamental split between whites opposed to improving conditions for blacks on the one hand and those in favor on the other, the linkages across specific racial issues are far looser today. These loose linkages show up in each of the three studies. The results from the National Election Study and the General Social Survey, at every point where detailed comparison is possible, match those from the Race and Politics survey. This consistency is important, for the closer the correspondence between the results from the national and the regional studies, the stronger the reason to conclude that crucial findings which will emerge in subsequent chapters apply not just to California but to the country as a whole.

What does the consistency of these results reveal about the place of race in American public life in the 1980s and 90s? What does the change that has taken place—the loosening of the ties binding one racial issue to another—reveal about the underlying forces shaping American attitudes on issues of race?

Most critically, racism no longer dominates the reactions of white Americans to issues of race across-the-board. Not very long ago—indeed, within the lifetime of most Americans who are now adults—the bulk of whites opposed any and every proposal to end racial inequality. They opposed integration; they opposed the notion that a black should be considered on the same terms as a white for a job, preferring instead that the jobs first go to whites and then—only if there was a surplus—should blacks get a chance; and they opposed the suggestion that the government ought to improve the social and economic conditions of blacks. Their opposition was ultimately rooted in a deep and visceral suspicion and hostility, in an unwillingness—in the last resort—to recognize and respect a black American as the equal of a white. Racial prejudice has not disappeared. But it no longer has the power to dominate the political thinking of ordinary Americans.

There is a measure of consistency in Americans' reactions to issues of race—it would be astonishing if there were not—and we shall go on in Chapters 4 and 5 to examine the different forms this consistency takes and the diverse factors that underlie it. Three points nonetheless deserve emphasis here. First, race prejudice is only one factor of many that induces a measure of consistency in a person's reaction to blacks and to policies designed to benefit blacks, and it is far from the most important; political ideology, to take the most obvious example, exerts a more decisive force. Second, consistency can take the form of either systematic opposition to a range of particular policies to assist blacks, or systematic support for them; and there is good reason to think that at least as many whites consistently line up in favor of policies to help blacks as consistently line up in opposition to them. And third, it is not true—not remotely close to being true—that the bulk of white Americans stand in opposition to policies to assist blacks issue after issue—and that, in itself, signals a fundamental and decisive transformation in the character of racial politics in America.

As part of this transformation, specific racial policies—whether government spending in behalf of blacks should be increased or not, for example, or whether school children should be bused to achieve racial integration—have become more complex. Rather than simply boiling down to how whites feel toward blacks, each of them now consists of a *bundle* of considerations. Some of these considerations are narrowly racial, hence influenced by people's feelings and beliefs about blacks. But others are not racial, having more to do with questions about what government should do and how it can best get done what it ought to do. Consider a specific racial policy issue such as how much effort the government should make to improve the economic and social conditions of blacks. As this issue typically is put to Americans, it manifestly wraps together diverse considerations:

> Some people think that the government in Washington should increase spending for programs to help blacks. Others feel that blacks should rely only on themselves. Which makes more sense to you? Should the government help improve the position of blacks, or should they rely only on themselves?

A variety of considerations are bundled together here, any or all of which may provide a basis for reaction. A person may choose a position on this issue on the basis of: (1) his attitude toward the federal government, favoring the idea of more spending if he broadly has confidence in the competence of the federal government, opposing it if he sees Washington as a sink of inefficiency and over-centralization; (2) his attitude toward government spending per se, favoring assistance for blacks if he broadly favors policies that entail, for their implementation, further government expenditures, opposing assistance if he believes government wastes too much of what it spends already; (3) his attitude toward blacks, favoring assistance for them if he feels sympathy for their circumstances, opposing it if he dislikes them; and (4) his attitude toward individual initiative and responsibility, favoring assistance for blacks if he believes that the magnitude of the problems facing blacks calls for government action, opposing it if he believes that progress requires individuals to accept responsibility for their own circumstances and take the primary responsibility for improving them. Plainly, a person could choose a position on the issue of government assistance for blacks—framed in terms of a choice between government spending and self-help—for any of these reasons; and some of these reasons have little or nothing intrinsically to do with race. They have instead to do with questions of politics and public policy that go beyond race. And just insofar as this is so, a central argument of this book is that the contemporary politics of race has as much to do with politics as with race.

If we are right, politics as well as race requires understanding. What can it mean to say that politics matters? It is useful, we think, to distinguish between two ways that politics can organize the contemporary conflict over issues of race. Politics may provide extrinsic or intrinsic constraints.

So far as the role of politics in issues of race has been recognized—and far and away the dominant tendency has been to omit it altogether—it is a source of extrinsic constraints. Thus, Carmines and Stimson's (1989) *Issue Evolution* argues that the rise of race as a public issue in American political life is rooted in the extrinsic dynamics of the American electoral system. The Republican party, they usefully remind us, used to be the party of racial tolerance; the Democratic party, if not in its creed then in its toleration of its southern wing, the party of segregation. But the parties reversed their field in 1964, with the presidential nominations of Lyndon Johnson for the Democrats and Barry Goldwater for the Republicans: the Democrats became the party of racial liberalism, the Republicans the party of racial conservatism. This sudden shift in the identification of the parties with racial liberalism and conservatism put race, in the minds of the electorate, at the center of political considerations.

From this point of view, political ideas can come together in the minds of citizens not because of an intrinsic connection among them but by virtue of temporal and political contiguity. The ordinary citizen, indifferent to politics most of the time, pays most attention in the course of presidential campaigns; the presidential candidates are the teachers—teaching what goes with what. This notion of the "time bundling of political issues" offers an important and persuasive reminder that how Americans' ideas about politics are organized reflects, in part, how American politics is organized. It also compellingly illustrates a classic lesson that the political logic of ideas reflects the vagaries and idiosyncracies of specific personalities and coalitions, disciplined by the competitive logic of a two-party system. But having said this, we also believe that the notion of time bundling represents only a partial and incomplete account of how politics itself helps organize the contemporary cleavage over race.

The politics of race is defined by an intrinsic as well as extrinsic logic, a logic imposed by the competing choices presented to the larger public. Every policy of race hinges on a choice between alternatives—alternative goals that should be sought, alternative means by which to accomplish them. And citizens' responses to those racial policies are shaped by the quite specific alternatives that they are asked to choose between. It makes a difference to citizens what a particular racial policy aims to accomplish and how it proposes to accomplish it. In taking a position on an issue like affirmative action or a larger role for government in improving the living conditions of blacks, they are, to be sure, reacting to the problem of race, but they are, more fundamentally, responding to specific choices put before them as to what government should and should not attempt. The differences of opinion between Americans over issues of race reflect cleavages that are partly racial but are still more fundamentally political.

At least three quite different kinds of choices are now before the American public. As we have seen, there is the cluster of racial policies with a New Deal flavor—policies that center on activist government, putting more resources or effort in the service of the disadvantaged. A paradigmatic example of this social welfare agenda is the proposal to increase government spending to assist blacks. This is a proposal that excites argument, partly—as previous research has emphasized—because it concerns blacks. But the argument is also about a *style* of public policy—and this is what previous research has failed to emphasize. The argument over social welfare policy is an argument of long standing, conducted in response to a variety of groups that are deprived or disadvantaged, and is by no means confined to blacks.

Manifestly distinguishable from the argument over the social welfare agenda is the current controversy over the race-conscious agenda. We are not suggesting that reactions to affirmative action are fastidiously divorced from the positions white Americans take on other issues of race. On the contrary, a decision to go forward and support racial quotas and preferential treatment carries with it an inclination to support most other less controversial and more familiar proposals to assist blacks. But it is all the same mistaken to reduce the argument over affirmative action to an argument over whether government should in any way assist blacks, let alone to an argument over whether the civil rights of blacks should be upheld. The response of Americans—black as well as white—to affirmative action has to be understood in its own right.

There is, finally, a set of issues we shall call the equal treatment agenda. The issue of race, at its core in the 1940s and 50s, centered on whether blacks were to be allowed to do what whites were permitted to do: Were blacks to be permitted to sit where they wished on a bus? Or to drink from the same water fountain that a white might touch? Or eat at the same table in a restaurant where a white might sit? The collapse of Jim Crow laws in the 1950s seemed to put the seal on the equal treatment agenda: at any rate as a matter of law, blacks formally had the same rights as whites.

It is widely believed that questions of equal treatment belong to the past. Americans, it is implied, accept equal treatment as public policy; they accept "color-blindness." What they balk at is race consciousness, in the form of affirmative action, quotas, set-asides, and other instances of preferential treatment for blacks. The notion is thus of a dynamic policy agenda, with older and more familiar forms of racial controversy being resolved and replaced by fresher and more controversial forms.

The *principle* of equal treatment has been accepted. In 1942, only a minority of white Americans opposed the statement that "there should be separate sections for Negroes in streetcars and buses"; by 1970, 88 percent were opposed. The legitimacy of official segregation—of laws enforcing the use of racially separate drinking fountains, public parks, restaurant facilities, and the like—has evaporated. This represents a sea change in American public life. Yet, it does not follow that all aspects of the equal treatment agenda have been settled. The issue of *government responsibility* to assure equal treatment for blacks remains, as we shall demonstrate in Chapter 5, very much a contested issue. It is by no means a settled principle that government should actively combat racial discrimination, and we shall take fair housing as a paradigmatic example of the issue of equal treatment. The evidence will show that the question of equal treatment as typified by the issue of fair housing not only remains closely contested but has to be understood in its own terms, not reduced to merely another item on either the social welfare or the race-conscious agenda.

REPRISE: THE POLITICS OF RACE

The contemporary American understanding of race has been defined by the politics of race at the peak of the civil rights movement. The cleavage over race, then, was deep but simple. Not only did many whites oppose policies to achieve racial equality, but their opposition showed itself across-the-board. It was not as though they took exception, say, to busing but found themselves willing to go along with, say, fair housing. Rather, they objected to the full range of policies to assist blacks, whatever the level of government to administer them, whatever the specific form of assistance to be given to blacks. And they objected to all of the policies because the particular policy was not the issue. *Blacks* were the issue; hence the famous dictum that the array of specific racial issues—in jobs, housing, education, and the like—all tended "to boil down to the same single question: Are you sympathetic to Negroes as a group, are you indifferent to them, or do you dislike them?"

And so far as issues dealing with blacks really did reduce to how people felt about blacks, the politics of race had a striking simplicity. The issue of race, at its heart, came down fundamentally to whether whites were prepared to accept blacks as their equals— whether, that is, whites were prepared to see blacks treated as they believe that they themselves should be treated. Now, however, the issue of race has become more complex—more complex because there are now multiple agendas. Whites no longer react uniformly to issues of race. Their views on racial policy depend partly on the policy itself—on whether it belongs on the social welfare, equal treatment, or race-conscious agenda.

To accept that conflicts over race are organized around policy agendas is to reject the traditional picture of racial politics as centered on one deep-lying cleavage between Americans who want to resist government efforts to help blacks because they despise and reject blacks and those who favor such government efforts because they accept and sympathize with blacks. Race continues to matter, but racism no longer dominates the policy preferences of whites.

This is not to say that whites' images and stereotypes of blacks do not shape in significant ways their responses to racial policies. On the contrary, in the next chapter we shall demonstrate in detail the continuing prevalence of negative evaluations of blacks, and later—in Chapters 4 and 5—we will show how the images whites hold of blacks shape their reactions to appeals for government action to assist blacks.

2

PICTURES IN
THE MIND

What do whites think about blacks? Undoubtedly, negative stereotypes about blacks were prevalent only a generation ago, but how common are they now? What are the negative stereotypes now attached to blacks: Do they take the form of a belief that blacks are inherently less intelligent and worthy than whites, or that blacks suffer from failings less of ability than of character? How widely diffused are racial stereotypes through contemporary American society? Are they found chiefly at its periphery—among the poor and poorly educated—or are they distributed more evenly, prevalent even among its more affluent and better educated parts? What do these negative stereotypes consist of at their core? To what extent are they a response to a person's encounters with blacks, a reaction to the world outside himself, to what extent are they driven by a person's own inner needs and conflicts? Are negative characterizations of blacks a product of ignorance and a lack of education or are they a product of the very values—self-reliance, hard work, individualism—on which Americans have prided themselves?

It would be natural to think that, nearly one half century after race emerged again as a front-row issue in American politics, much is known about the answers to these questions. Haven't national surveys routinely documented the prevalence of negative racial stereotypes, their principal points of concentration in the larger American society, and their direct impact on the positions that white Americans take on issues of race? In fact, little has been done. Roughly from the 1950s until the 1990s, what is conspicuous in national public opinion surveys is not the measurement of racial stereotypes but its absence.

Partly owing to the dearth of reliable information, a mythology has grown up around the problem of racial stereotypes. Perhaps the most crucial of these myths expresses itself in the ubiquitous assumption that whites no longer will openly express a frankly derogatory characterization of blacks—certainly not when talking to a stranger. A generation ago, many whites indisputably felt that blacks were inferior, and felt at liberty to say so. What has changed, it is suggested, is not how they feel toward blacks but what they feel free to say about them. Who, it is asked, will make an explicitly derogatory statement about blacks to a stranger? Who will openly make remarks that could give the impression they are racists?

A genuine change has taken place in American attitudes toward race over the last half century, above all in the collapse of popular support for *de jure* racial segregation. This change should not be minimized, not least because it underlines the potential for education and improvement, but neither should it be exaggerated. The open expression of frankly negative characterizations of blacks, without question, is frowned on at many times and in some places. But if one goes out into American society and talks with taxi drivers or nurses or transportation executives or schoolteachers or a host of others about problems of race in American life, one would have to put blinders on one's eyes and cotton batten in one's ears not to see and hear the negative characterizations routinely expressed about blacks. Accordingly, one of the principal objectives of this chapter is to demonstrate that negative characterizations of blacks remain prevalent in contemporary American society notwithstanding the changes that have taken place, and that, contrary to the conventional wisdom, these negative racial characterizations are openly and routinely expressed.

A second objective is to establish some of the sources of racial stereotypes. Why do many whites believe that blacks could be as well-off as whites if they only applied themselves? Or say that blacks take advantage of welfare? Or that they fail to take care of their homes and neighborhoods? To what extent are these negative characterizations of blacks driven by a person's actual experience with blacks? To what extent are they an expression not of a person's feelings toward blacks specifically but instead his or her reactions to outgroups generally, whatever their race, religion, or ethnicity?

We shall demonstrate that negative racial stereotypes remain embedded in a broader tendency to derogate an array of outgroups, not just blacks. In particular, we will show that the person who believes that most Jews engage in shady practices and that Jews are indifferent to the well-being of those who are not Jewish tends also to believe that most blacks have a chip on their shoulder and take advantage of welfare. Without denying that other factors play a part, we want to insist that one cannot grasp the psychology of racial stereotypes without understanding that the best way to predict if a person will endorse a negative characterization of blacks is to know if he or she has endorsed a negative characterization of Jews. That dislike of Jews is tied so closely to dislike of blacks—two groups whose history and circumstances are so different in so many ways—ought to make palpable the irrationality of intolerance, whether racial or religious. Moreover, the continuing entanglement of anti-Jewish and antiblack beliefs serves as a reminder that the psychology of racial stereotypes at its core is much the same now as a generation ago, notwithstanding the suggestion so frequently bruited about that an altogether new kind of racism, more polite and more mainstream than the old, is now on the scene.

Our third objective in this chapter is to explore the relation of racial stereotypes to traditional American values. To explain how racism has cohabited with liberal democracy, two answers typically have been given. Following Myrdal, one answer treats American slavery and racism as an anomaly—an accident of history, a product of factors exogenous to liberal democracy. The other answer treats the "apparent anomaly," in Jennifer Hochschild's words, as an "actual symbiosis"—as an immanent corollary of the political and economic values central to liberal democracy. The sheer persistence of the problem of race has suggested to an increasing number of scholars that racism is built in to the American experience; indeed, as many have come to conclude, it is the inescapable, if unintended, product of values long regarded as distinctively, even quintessentially, American—values such as personal autonomy, hard work, self-discipline, achievement. If this claim is true, and many scholars have concluded that it is, then racism is truly as American as apple pie.

The connection between traditional American values and race prejudice, although it has seemed to many commentators to be straightforward, is in fact subtle—subtle because the notion of traditional values in a liberal society is itself subtle. We shall show that there has been a terrible confusion of two different notions of traditional values, a running together of individualistic values on the one side and authoritarian ones on the other. All too commonly, some whites declare that blacks fail to work hard and to stand on their own two feet. But it is a great mistake to assume, as commentators on race and public affairs often have, that the person who says that blacks attach too little importance to achievement and effort attaches great importance to standing on his own two feet and exercising initiative, industry, and perseverance in his own life. Those are the criteria by which he judges others, not himself. Instead, what sets him apart, as we shall show, is the importance that he attaches to authority, obedience, and conformity. What underlies perceptions of blacks as lacking a willingness to work hard is thus not the ethic of hard work associated with individualism but the ethic of discipline and conformity associated with authoritarianism.

NEGATIVE CHARACTERIZATIONS OF BLACKS

Do whites see blacks as hard-working, responsible, trustworthy, or as lazy, self-destructive, violent? How negative, how hostile, are white attitudes toward blacks? Questions like these, it is sometimes suggested, are out of reach. Racism, it is asserted, is no longer blatant: people nowadays are reluctant to express openly their dislike of and contempt for blacks, indeed, are not prepared to express publicly a sentiment that could be interpreted as racist. Racism, it is said, is "subtle": it is disguised, kept out of sight.

This line of argument has intuitive appeal: it fits our common-sense understanding that people tailor their words and deeds to their social circumstances, concealing ideas or attributes that would evoke disapproval, were others in a position to detect them. And systematic research complements common sense. For example, as Crosby and her colleagues have observed, whites express more favorable attitudes toward blacks when they are speaking to a black interviewer, more negative attitudes when they are speaking to a white interviewer. Analogously, if whites are persuaded that a lie on their part will be detected by the interviewer, they are more likely to admit to harboring negative feelings about blacks. Plainly, the level of hostility expressed against blacks is not a constant but varies from situation to situation, receding from sight when it would evoke social criticism and disapproval, looming larger when it appears that an antiblack response would be permitted or even when it is merely uncertain that it would be prohibited. We would obviously be unreasonable to expect bigots always to express their hostility against blacks, let alone always to express it to the fullest extent.

The notion of subtle racism so closely conforms to thoughtful people's intuitions about human nature that it seems not simply true but self-evidently so. It is, however, important to think it through carefully, not least because the very desire to call attention to the problem of prejudice can have the effect, as we shall show, of minimizing its prevalence.

Consider the logic underlying the notion of subtle racism. The assertion that racism nowadays cannot be expressed openly and overtly but must instead be disguised presupposes the existence of strong social norms against the expression of frankly negative evaluations of blacks. But how compelling, one must ask, is the presupposition of a problack societal norm?

To obtain some sense of the willingness of whites to make derogatory assertions about blacks, we presented respondents with a variety of negative characterizations of blacks. These included assertions that blacks were inherently inferior to whites, inclined to exploit welfare, unwilling to work hard, irresponsible, belligerent, and violent. To begin with the most encouraging result, consider whites' reactions to a suggestion that blacks are innately inferior to whites. As part of a series of questions directed at determining why the average black American is not as well off as the average white American, we asked if the reason is that:

Blacks are born with less ability.

Only 6 percent of whites concur with the characterization of blacks as inherently less intelligent and able than whites. This is a strikingly small number by any standard. Even as recently as fifteen years ago, 23 percent of whites in the San Francisco-Oakland Bay Area declared that the average black was not as well off as the average white because blacks are born with less ability. And the contrast between American racial attitudes at the end of the 1940s, when assertions of the innate inferiority of blacks were commonplace, and at the end of the 1980s, when such views were mouthed by only a relative handful, is like the difference between night and day. But without minimizing the importance of this change, it by no means follows that negative characterizations of blacks have disappeared. On the contrary, what is striking about the results we see in the chart on page 41 is not how few but rather how many whites endorse a range of negative characterizations of blacks. Thus, at the opposite extreme from the stereotype of innate black inferiority, which is rare, is the perception of blacks' taking advantage of government assistance, which is anything but rare. By way of getting a grip on this stereotype, we asked respondents if they agreed that:

Most blacks who are on welfare programs could get a job if they really tried.

Notice that we did not ask if "some" blacks on welfare could find a job and support themselves; we asked instead whether "most" of them could get a job—a rather different proposition. Yet the response to this negative characterization of blacks is at the opposite end of the spectrum from the response to assertions of inherent black inferiority. Whereas only a tiny percentage endorse the view that blacks are born less able than whites, a clear-cut majority—61 percent—believe that most blacks on welfare could find work if they wanted to.

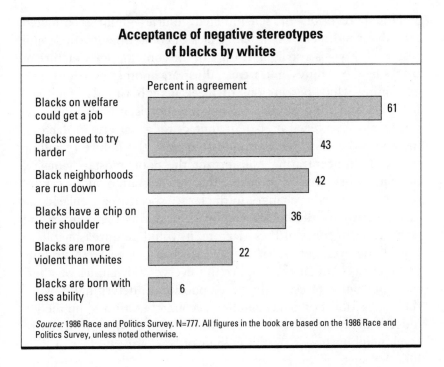

Acceptance of negative stereotypes of blacks by whites

Percent in agreement

Blacks on welfare could get a job	61
Blacks need to try harder	43
Black neighborhoods are run down	42
Blacks have a chip on their shoulder	36
Blacks are more violent than whites	22
Blacks are born with less ability	6

Source: 1986 Race and Politics Survey. N=777. All figures in the book are based on the 1986 Race and Politics Survey, unless noted otherwise.

Moreover, the belief that blacks on welfare are taking advantage of the program is only one instance of a cluster of beliefs which accent a lack of effort, initiative, self-reliance, and responsibility on the part of blacks. By way of exploring this broader cluster of beliefs, we also asked whites if they basically agreed or disagreed that:

If blacks would only try harder, they would be just as well off as whites.

Almost one in every two agreed.

Whites clearly perceive blacks to be contributing to the problems that plague them. It is not that they believe blacks are responsible for the problems having arisen in the first place. On the contrary, two in every three whites in the Race and Politics Survey agree that a history of slavery and being discriminated against have created conditions that make it difficult for black people to work their way up. But although many whites are ready to acknowledge that whites were originally responsible for blacks' problems, and even though many of them believe that this past still has a bearing on the present, large numbers of whites also perceive blacks to be making their own circumstances worse.

This perception of self-inflicted injuries—injuries inflicted directly or indirectly because of a lack of commitment, effort, and responsibility—is a striking feature of the contemporary picture of blacks held by whites, and we can illustrate another aspect of it by examining white perceptions of black neighborhoods. The violence and squalor of some black neighborhoods, it is obvious to an impartial observer, can be attributed to a variety of factors, including the loss of urban industrial jobs, the failure of public policy (in concentrating housing for the poor, most obviously), discriminatory lending policies, the out-migration of successful blacks, and broader changes in the larger society, particularly the disintegration of the nuclear family. Considering the number and complexity of some of these factors, it would be unreasonable to expect the average citizen to have worked out an appropriately complex account of the origins and everyday dynamics of ghettoes. But our interest is the very opposite: to determine how far they subscribe not to a complex account but to a simplified—indeed, oversimplified—account which blames the problems of black neighborhoods on the failings of blacks themselves. To see how far such an oversimplified account would be endorsed, we asked respondents if they agreed or disagreed that:

> Black neighborhoods tend to be run down because blacks simply don't take care of their property.

This assertion carries quietly with it the implicit contention that black neighborhoods are run down because they are black; and one might be forgiven for supposing that this contention would inspire—in conversation with a stranger—some objection, with people taking the position, for example, that a crucial consideration was not whether a neighborhood was black but rather whether it was poor. But notwithstanding these and other reasons to disagree, again almost one in every two whites adopts this moralistic and one-sided account, agreeing (either strongly or somewhat) that the problem is that blacks simply don't take care of their own property.

A perception of a lack of effort and responsibility, of the absence of a willingness to do the best one can in an admittedly difficult situation, has arguably become the most prominent feature of negative perceptions of blacks now. But it is by no means the only instance of perceived black behavior to which substantial numbers of whites take exception. Another, for example, is a perception of blacks as belligerent. Consider the following characterization:

Most blacks have a chip on their shoulder.

Granted that many young inner-city male blacks act tough, striking a belligerent, aggressive posture in the company of whites; to perceive them as having a chip on their shoulder is no more than to perceive reality as it actually is. But this characterization was not specifically aimed at "young male ghetto blacks," or at "young male blacks," or even at "young blacks." And however the behavior and demeanor of many young ghetto males should be characterized, it is a stretch to argue that *most* blacks—women as well as men, over sixty as well as under twenty, in the suburbs as well as in the cities—are conspicuously and distinctively truculent. All the same, 36 percent of all whites—approximately one in every three—agree (strongly or somewhat) that most blacks have a chip on their shoulder.

This perception of blacks as belligerent and resentful, though no doubt reflecting in part a belief that blacks are not managing the responsibility common to everyone to behave decently and exercise self-control even in trying circumstances, also betrays an uneasiness and concern for personal safety on the part of whites. Thus, we asked whether:

Blacks are more violent than whites.

About one in every five whites agreed.

Does it follow that whites who agreed that blacks are more violent—or, for that matter, those who agreed blacks are taking advantage of welfare or are not trying as hard as they could to get ahead—are racial bigots? Is agreement with a negative characterization, in and of itself, proof of prejudice?

All of these negative characterizations of blacks are fed by prejudice, as we shall show. But apart only from the characterization of blacks as inherently inferior to whites, they cannot be entirely reduced to bigotry, for these characterizations capture real features of everyday experience. For example, the perception of blacks as more violent than whites, and in particular the apprehension about young black males as more prone to criminal conduct, has an element of reality to it. Although blacks are only slightly more than one in every ten in the population as a whole, in 1990 they were responsible for one in every two murders, and in 1989 for more than six in every ten robberies. The common perception of the disintegration of the nuclear family among blacks is also rooted in reality. In 1988, 63.7 percent of black births were out of wedlock, the figure being higher still in urban areas, and in 1990, 56.2 percent of black households were headed by women, the majority of whom had never been married. Nor is the common perception that blacks do not do well at school without a kernel of truth. The average Scholastic Aptitude Test score of blacks, in 1990, was 737, compared with an average white score of 993; and still more disturbing, the picture does not materially brighten if differences in income are taken into account. Even black students from well-off homes do not do well on standardized tests of academic aptitude; indeed, as Andrew Hacker has remarked, blacks "whose parents earn between $50,000 and $60,000 barely match Asians from families in the $10,000 to $20,000 range."

A person who is concerned about racial intolerance and the injustices it has inspired has difficulty accepting the notion that a negative characterization, merely by virtue of being negative, is not a sign of prejudice, still more so accepting the suggestion that many of these negative characterizations have an element of truth to them. Examining the reactions of whites to blacks in isolation, which is the way it has always been done in the past, obscures the depth of the problem of race. What blacks think of blacks also needs to be taken into account.

Taking advantage of a national survey conducted in 1991, we are in a position to do this for the first time. Everyone interviewed in the course of this study, whether black or white, was asked to describe what blacks as a group are like. A number of adjectives were read—for example, aggressive or violent, boastful, and irresponsible—with respondents indicating how well each adjective described blacks by picking a number from 0 to 10, the higher the number, the better or more accurate the description. The chart on page 45 compares the reactions of whites and blacks.

Plainly, large numbers of whites are perfectly willing to express frankly negative evaluations of blacks. At least one in every two perceives blacks as a group to be aggressive or violent, and nearly as

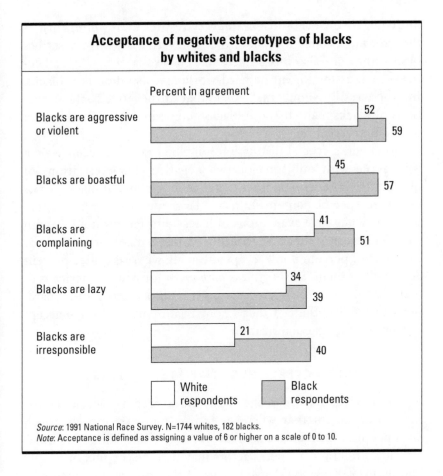

Acceptance of negative stereotypes of blacks by whites and blacks

Percent in agreement

Blacks are aggressive or violent
White: 52
Black: 59

Blacks are boastful
White: 45
Black: 57

Blacks are complaining
White: 41
Black: 51

Blacks are lazy
White: 34
Black: 39

Blacks are irresponsible
White: 21
Black: 40

☐ White respondents   ▨ Black respondents

Source: 1991 National Race Survey. N=1744 whites, 182 blacks.
Note: Acceptance is defined as assigning a value of 6 or higher on a scale of 0 to 10.

many are ready to describe blacks as boastful and complaining. The national results thus confirm the RAP findings. But the national study adds a new element altogether. In every case blacks are at least as likely as whites to hold a negative view of blacks. For example, 52 percent of white respondents describe blacks as aggressive or violent; for black respondents, the number is 59 percent. For white respondents, 34 percent describe blacks as lazy; the number among black respondents is 39 percent. Indeed, when it comes to judgments of whether blacks as a group exhibit socially undesirable characteristics, whenever there is a statistically significant difference between the views of blacks and whites, it *always* takes the form of blacks expressing a more negative evaluation of other blacks than do whites. It is not true that blacks have a more negative view of blacks in every respect than whites. Just as they are more likely to believe that a negative adjective describes blacks, they are also more likely to believe that a positive adjective—such as intelligent or hard-working—also describes blacks. But these results should make plain that the negative characterizations of blacks made by both blacks and whites are rooted in part in a common reality.

Moreover, a crucial distinction must be drawn between people who agree with only one or two negative characterizations of blacks and those who endorse negative judgments of blacks whatever their specific content. In fact, a large number of whites agree with a few negative evaluations of blacks, but far fewer agree with a large number of them. Specifically, 39 percent accept only one or two, and 22 percent don't accept any at all, whereas only 2 percent accept all of them. In short, it is *uncommon* for white Americans to endorse negative characterizations of blacks across-the-board, notwithstanding the fact that a nontrivial number of them accept one or another characterization.

WHO ACCEPTS NEGATIVE STEREOTYPES?

A substantial and distinguished body of research has developed the general argument that whatever factors put a person "in touch with people whose ideas and values are different from one's own" promotes tolerance. These factors may include the mix of people and points of view in a person's part of the country, or the mix he or she is exposed to through traveling, or by taking part in politics, or—and this was once a theme—through the process of education. The more schooling people have had, the greater the likelihood that they will be exposed to, and be able to understand, the core values and official norms of American culture—values and norms that centrally include the principle of tolerance itself. So far as this is true, then whatever moves a person toward the center of American society and away from its periphery should promote all the varieties of tolerance—political, religious, and racial, too.

Not that all aspects of a person's social standing are of equal importance in promoting tolerance. The amount of formal schooling that one has had should count for a lot, while the amount of money one makes should count for little—except insofar as it is correlated with the amount of education one has had. After all, the better educated, by virtue of being better informed, more adept at picking up and processing information, and better able to handle abstract ideas, are more likely to have a grip on the official norms of the larger culture, which in the case of the United States prominently include tolerance. No less important, by virtue of both the immediate and the longer-run benefits of schooling, the better educated are better positioned to recognize when a sentiment that they encounter in their everyday interactions violates the norms of the larger society, and, recognizing this, more likely to reject sentiments that are offensive, punitive, or otherwise intolerant. In contrast, it is not obvious why having more money, or enjoying more social status, by themselves, should incline one to be open-minded and tolerant, and indeed, much in the way of historical experience counsels otherwise.

Factors other than formal schooling surely influence the likelihood that people will accept one or another negative characterization of blacks. Most obviously, contemporary American society is divided by ideological outlook, with liberals differing systematically from conservatives. We do not mean to overstress the role of ideas in political life, still less that of ideology, but previous research has made plain that one determinant of how ordinary Americans react to questions of race is ideology.

By way of getting a sense of the extent to which acceptance of negative characterizations of blacks is tied to people's social location and ideological outlook, we looked at the correlations between the number of negative racial characterizations they accept and their age, family income, years of schooling, and ideological self-identification.

Consider first the factors that turn out to be unimportant. Common sense might suggest that negative reactions to blacks are driven by anxiety and resentment and hence should be most common among the have-nots and have-littles. For that matter, it may seem obvious that a more negative perception of blacks is nearly a signature characteristic of older Americans, raised in a different climate of opinion. But as the chart on page 48 shows, neither family income nor age has much to do with acceptance of negative racial stereotypes. In contrast with results from the 1950s and 60s, which showed that young adults tended to be more open-

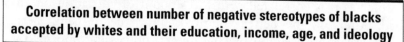

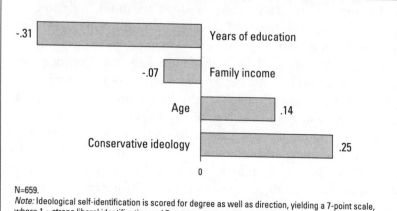

Correlation between number of negative stereotypes of blacks accepted by whites and their education, income, age, and ideology

-.31 — Years of education

-.07 — Family income

Age — .14

Conservative ideology — .25

0

N=659.
Note: Ideological self-identification is scored for degree as well as direction, yielding a 7-point scale, where 1 = strong liberal identification and 7 = strong conservative identification. Income is measured by eleven categories, ranging from under $15,000 per year to over $50,000 per year.

minded than the older ones they were replacing, our results suggest that the process of increasing societal tolerance with each new generation has, at least for the moment, come to an end.

But if age and income do not matter, education manifestly does. The number of years of schooling a person has had is significantly related to the number of negative characterizations about blacks that he or she accepts: as schooling goes up, acceptance of negative characterizations goes down. In addition, ideological orientation also makes a difference. The more liberal people perceive themselves to be, the fewer negative racial characterizations they are likely to endorse, while the more conservative they perceive themselves to be, the more negative characterizations they are likely to accept.

But how, exactly, do education and ideology work together? And what difference does either, or both, make to the overall willingness of whites to accept the most common stereotypes about blacks? As the chart on page 49 shows, for nearly every combination of education and ideology, the majority belief among whites is that most blacks on welfare could get a job if they really tried.

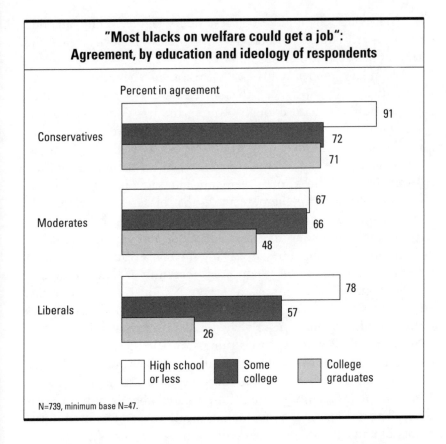

"Most blacks on welfare could get a job":
Agreement, by education and ideology of respondents

Percent in agreement

Conservatives
- 91
- 72
- 71

Moderates
- 67
- 66
- 48

Liberals
- 78
- 57
- 26

High school or less   Some college   College graduates

N=739, minimum base N=47.

Among respondents with at most a high school degree, conservatives and liberals are both overwhelmingly likely to perceive blacks as taking advantage of welfare: 91 percent of the less-educated conservatives and 78 percent of less-educated liberals agree that most blacks on welfare are exploiting it. The overall proportion of whites perceiving blacks as exploitative steadily drops the more formal schooling whites have had—from approximately eight in ten among the least educated to six in ten among the moderately educated, to five in ten among the most. But describing the variation this way conceals as much as it reveals, for increases in formal schooling undercut popular support for this stereotype chiefly among people who see themselves as liberal in outlook. Among well-educated conservatives, 71 percent still perceive blacks as taking advantage of welfare, and for that matter nearly 50 percent of well-educated middle-of-the-roaders agree. Only in one group—well-educated liberals—does a clear majority *reject* the view of blacks as exploiting welfare.

A similar pattern holds for diffusion of the other negative stereotypes—for instance, that blacks are poor because they simply don't try hard enough. Among the less educated, liberals are statistically as likely as conservatives to believe that if blacks would only try harder, they would be just as well-off as whites. Once again, the higher a person's level of formal education, the lower his or her level of agreement. The same pattern of distribution holds also for the perception that blacks are irresponsible and do not take care of their neighborhoods, with the stereotype most common among the least educated (and among them, just as common among liberals as among conservatives) and least common among the most educated—certainly if they are liberal.

An identical analysis of the 1986 National Election Study, focusing on the perception of blacks as failing to try as hard as they could or should, yields virtually identical results. In both the NES and RAP studies, three things are significant: (1) the less educated people are, the more negative are their images of blacks; (2) the more conservative, the more negative are their images of blacks; and (3) the images that less-educated liberals and conservatives have of blacks are much alike, while those of well-educated liberals and conservatives markedly differ.

What does this pattern of results signify? What does it reveal about the diffusion of negative racial stereotypes in contemporary American life? First, the cleavage over images of blacks is more, not less, pronounced among the more aware and better educated citizens. But the reason for this is not because educated conservatives have an especially negative view of blacks, but rather because educated liberals have an especially positive view. Second, with the exception only of citizens who are uncommonly well educated and uncommonly liberal, what is striking is the sheer pervasiveness throughout contemporary American society of negative characterizations of blacks—particularly the stereotype that most blacks on welfare could get a job. Perceptions of blacks as inferior were supposed to represent an archaic stock of beliefs that were in the process of dying out, and some indeed do appear to be fading out. But it completely misreads contemporary American culture to suppose that all negative characterizations of blacks are dwindling away. On the contrary, images of blacks as failing to make a genuine effort to work hard and to deal responsibly with their obligations is a standard belief throughout most of American society. Only among the relatively small segment characterized both by extensive education and a liberal outlook on politics is it rejected by large numbers. We read these results as suggesting that, notwithstanding the role of societal institutions like formal schooling in reducing the prevalence of negative racial stereotypes, negative stereotypes of blacks' character are widely diffused through contemporary American society. Indeed, for these stereotypes to be rejected may be more the exception than the rule.

Insofar as negative stereotypes of blacks continue to be widely diffused, it is all the more important to uncover what underlies them. What factors are responsible for whites' perceiving blacks to be unwilling to make a genuine effort to deal with their problems? Obviously, any specific person can agree with an antiblack characterization for a multitude of reasons, some idiosyncratic to his or her experience. What we are interested in is uncovering a primary factor that explains why some whites systematically and consistently react negatively to blacks.

THE PSYCHOLOGY OF PREJUDICE

Consider a specific stereotype—say, that blacks are more violent than whites. Agreement with this characterization may be an expression of prejudice, but it need not be. Someone, having read the newspapers and watched television over a period of years, may agree because the stereotype of black violence fits consistently the stream of information from the mass media to which they have been exposed. Or a person may accept the negative characterization because it fits accurately his or her personal experience, or, yet again, because it fits with objective social indicators—for example, published rates on violent crime. Moreover, the attribution of a negative characteristic to blacks need not signal a negative feeling toward them. To acquiesce in a characterization of blacks as more violent than whites may be the handiwork of bigotry, but, alternatively, it may reflect a conviction that blacks continue to be victimized by a racist society, and the brutality that some blacks exhibit is itself the product of a society that has brutalized them. Everyone who accepts a negative stereotype about blacks is not prejudiced, and still more to the point, some who accept a negative stereotype about blacks are sympathetic, not hostile, to blacks and supportive of policies to help them. But acknowledging this, can we tell if prejudice plays, if not a completely determinative, then at any rate a manifestly important role in fostering stereotypes of blacks?

Two works opened up the modern study of prejudice and politics—*An American Dilemma* by Gunnar Myrdal, which we have already mentioned, and *The Authoritarian Personality* by Theodor Adorno, Else Frenkel-Brunswik, Daniel Levinson, and Nevitt Sanford. *An American Dilemma* sparked relatively little follow-up research but became a central plank of the broader intellectual culture in America. *The Authoritarian Personality* inspired a generation of research and has sunk from sight. It is time, we think, to call attention again to the latter's analysis of the psychology of prejudice.

The argument of Adorno and his colleagues is complexly woven together from many threads of evidence, but its two principal strands can be succinctly set out. The first is the "personality" thesis. Prejudice, according to the personality thesis, is rooted in part in people's most deep-seated psychological needs and conflicts—rooted, that is, in basic and enduring aspects of their personality, established early in childhood, primarily in response to their parents, particularly in reaction to punitive fathers and overbearing mothers.

The second strand of the argument—the strand which has received the least attention but which deserves the most emphasis—is the concept of ethnocentrism. This concept was introduced by William Graham Sumner and defined as "the technical name for the view of things in which one's own group is the center of everything. Each group nourishes its own pride and vanity and boasts itself superior and looks with contempt on outsiders." The idea of ethnocentrism was reoriented by Adorno and his colleagues to deemphasize the idealization of a person's own group, in favor of accentuating the denigration of groups he considers inferior. Ethnocentrism, so conceived, refers to the systematic tendency on the part of prejudiced individuals to dislike and derogate other ethnic groups across-the-board. Racial prejudice is thus, in a literal sense, a blind and irrational reaction against blacks, blind and irrational because it has nothing intrinsically to do with blacks and may just as well manifest itself against Jews, or Asians, or any of many outgroups.

Ethnocentrism, we want to suggest, offers a key to the irrationality of some current negative stereotypes about blacks. Adorno and his colleagues demonstrated the irrationality of anti-Semitism by showing that negative stereotypes about Jews are part of a larger syndrome of prejudice against blacks· and others. Inverting their logic, we shall demonstrate the irrationality of prejudice against blacks by showing that negative stereotypes about blacks are part of a larger syndrome of prejudice, one element of which is anti-Semitism.

In defining prejudice as a tendency to denigrate outgroups, and not blacks solely, we are in no way implying that different outgroups are subjected to the same level of prejudice. We are not suggesting that Jews nowadays are as frequently beset by prejudice as blacks—they are not. But we are insisting that the readiness to derogate outgroups tends to be general: an irrational dislike of blacks tends to go hand in hand with dislike of Jews.

A generation ago, negative stereotyping of blacks was decidedly an aspect of a broader ethnocentrism. Now, there is talk of a "new racism." What we shall demonstrate, on the contrary, is that racial prejudice remains the same old racism at its core, as evidenced by the fact that negative stereotyping of blacks now, just as before, is embedded in a larger pattern of ethnocentrism.

The crucial datum is the consistency of reactions to outgroups. We shall explore three negative stereotypes of Jews, drawn from seminal studies of anti-Semitism conducted by Charles Y. Glock, Gertrude Selznick, and their colleagues.

> Jews are more willing than others to use shady practices to get ahead.
> Most Jews don't care what happens to people who aren't Jewish.
> Most Jews are pushy.

In response to each of these negative characterizations of Jews, respondents were asked whether they agreed strongly, agreed somewhat, disagreed somewhat, or disagreed strongly. What is striking is that people's reactions to black stereotypes are highly predictable on the basis of their reactions to Jewish stereotypes, and vice versa, as the chart on page 54 makes plain. The person

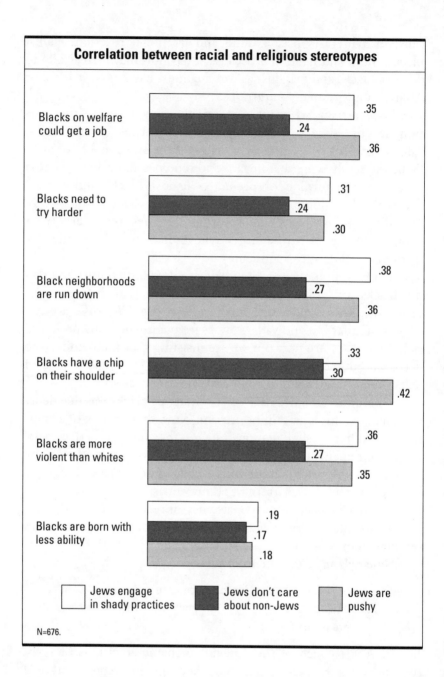

Correlation between racial and religious stereotypes

Blacks on welfare could get a job
- Jews engage in shady practices: .35
- Jews don't care about non-Jews: .24
- Jews are pushy: .36

Blacks need to try harder
- Jews engage in shady practices: .31
- Jews don't care about non-Jews: .24
- Jews are pushy: .30

Black neighborhoods are run down
- Jews engage in shady practices: .38
- Jews don't care about non-Jews: .27
- Jews are pushy: .36

Blacks have a chip on their shoulder
- Jews engage in shady practices: .33
- Jews don't care about non-Jews: .30
- Jews are pushy: .42

Blacks are more violent than whites
- Jews engage in shady practices: .36
- Jews don't care about non-Jews: .27
- Jews are pushy: .35

Blacks are born with less ability
- Jews engage in shady practices: .19
- Jews don't care about non-Jews: .17
- Jews are pushy: .18

Jews engage in shady practices   Jews don't care about non-Jews   Jews are pushy

N=676.

who says that Jews are pushy is a good bet to say that blacks have a chip on their shoulder, and the one who says that Jews use shady practices is an excellent bet to believe that blacks don't take care of their neighborhoods. Simply put, a response to any given question about Jews allows us to predict the response to any given question about blacks very nearly as well as another question actually about blacks.

Consistency is the mark of prejudice; indeed, by prejudice we mean explicitly the tendency systematically to respond negatively to outgroups. Thus, although a large number of whites endorse a few negative characterizations of blacks, only a much smaller number agree with many of them, and most of them are the very same people who agree with a large number of negative character- izations of Jews. For example, 84 percent of whites who agree with all six negative stereotypes about blacks agree with at least two out of three anti-Semitic items; conversely, only 10 percent of those who agree with only one negative characterization of blacks agree with two out of three anti-Semitic items.

But has the syndrome of ethnocentrism, first demonstrated to exist one half century ago, maintained its coherence and strength in all parts of contemporary American society? Is it perhaps on the defensive, if not in the society as a whole, then at least among those who have had the advantage of education and of growing up in a more tolerant climate of opinion? The question is not whether education, for example, works against acceptance of neg- ative stereotypes of either blacks or Jews—it does—but rather whether a person who succumbs to accepting stereotypes about one outgroup in spite of being well educated will go on to accept negative stereotypes about another outgroup.

As the chart on page 56 shows, whether people have barely made it out of high school or have graduated from college, whether they are just starting out, in their thirties, or are more mature, say, in their fifties or older, they will tend to espouse antiblack stereotypes if they espouse anti-Jewish stereotypes, and vice versa. This suggests that the psychology of racial prejudice is not as socially malleable as is often supposed. The tendency to respond in a systematic way to outgroups is not inhibited by one's social circumstances or standing and is as marked among the most educated and best off as among the least educated and worst off.

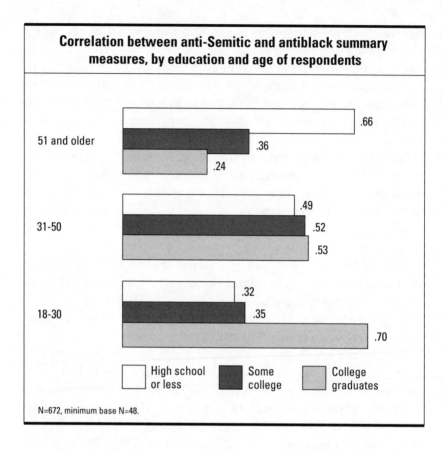

Correlation between anti-Semitic and antiblack summary measures, by education and age of respondents

51 and older
- High school or less: .66
- Some college: .36
- College graduates: .24

31-50
- High school or less: .49
- Some college: .52
- College graduates: .53

18-30
- High school or less: .32
- Some college: .35
- College graduates: .70

☐ High school or less   ■ Some college   ▨ College graduates

N=672, minimum base N=48.

These findings suggest strongly that racism today is the same old racism: ethnocentrism is its mark now as much as ever, and not only on average but across quite different parts of American society.

But perhaps there is a new racism in a different sense, still benefiting from its customary sources of support but now given a new lease on life by virtue of tapping new reservoirs in American society and culture?

THE NEW RACISM

To discuss the place of racism in American politics is to take part in a larger discussion about the nature of the American experience itself. It is an experience which generations of commentators saw as democratic and egalitarian at its heart. The American ethos was certainly not free of imperfection: the willingness to defend the rights of unpopular groups to speak and meet was deeply qualified, and obviously a variety of forms of prejudice—of racial bigotry, nativism, anti-Semitism—have continued to stain American politics. But it was always possible, and indeed customary, to see the imperfections as evidence of historical factors, the product of external or contingent circumstances, not the direct and logical product of the American ethos itself. According to this view, race prejudice has steadily lost ground as the fundamental American ideas of fair play, justice, and equality have gradually won the upper hand.

But the liberal optimism of Gunnar Myrdal and fellow commentators on race and American society a generation ago is today being attacked by some researchers. Racism, they argue, only appears to be on the defensive; indeed, at the very moment it appeared to have irretrievably lost ground, it disguised itself and now maintains as strong a grip on the thinking of white Americans as ever. The new racism, they thus argue, is not a product of beliefs either marginal to, or at odds with, the American Creed, as Myrdal supposed. Rather, its wellspring has proven to be precisely those traditional values emblematic of the American experience.

The suggestion that race prejudice continues to thrive because it is built-in to the American ethos itself is the central plank in the argument that a new racism has been born. Its proponents, whatever other points on which they disagree, all agree that the new racism is rooted in a "conjunction" of antiblack feeling and the kind of traditional values embodied in the Protestant ethic, including "hard work, individualism, sexual repression, and delay of gratification, with large doses of patriotism and reverence for the past thrown in." The overall thrust of the definition is clear, although the details may seem, on examination, to be less than compelling. It is one thing to speak of individualism as a traditional American value, but it is by no means obvious in what sense sexual repression is a quintessentially American value. If it was bound up with a particular Protestant conception of the Creed, most evident at the founding three centuries ago, it is hard to say with a straight face that contemporary American culture is centrally characterized by a commitment to sexual repression. Nor, in a popular culture as given to hurly-burly as the American, is it at all obvious what it means to say that reverence for the past is a distinctively American value. Reverence for all aspects of the past?

For certain symbolic aspects associated with the founding of the political order?

We do not mean to get caught up in quibbles. The larger problem here is that the new racism researchers have advanced a conception of traditional American values which gets wrong just what is most distinctive about them. As Louis Hartz argued a generation ago, the absolutely indispensable point to grasp is that "traditional," in the American context, can be a synonym for "liberal," in the sense of favoring individual freedom of action or expression. Not all traditional values are liberal, but one cannot understand the trajectory of the American experience without understanding that, in America, the tradition is liberal. By contrast, racism nowadays is said—as a matter of definition—to represent "a form of resistance to change in the racial status quo based on moral feelings that blacks violate such traditional American values as individualism and self-reliance, the work ethic, obedience, and discipline." But this definition of traditional American values joins together, purely by fiat, two sets of readily distinguishable values—individualism, self-reliance, and the work ethic on the one side, obedience and discipline on the other. What do these two sets of values have to do with each other?

A clear distinction can and ought to be made between the place of a value like individualism and a value like discipline in the American culture, or in broader terms, between individualistic values and authoritarian ones. Individualism can fairly be described in the American setting as a traditional value, but in the special sense that Hartz meant, as bound up with a liberal tradition. The second set of values—obedience and discipline—has an altogether different standing in American culture. Who ever supposed that obedience was a characteristic that Americans either exhibited to an uncommon degree or held in uncommon esteem? And what about discipline? It may make sense to say that discipline is a German value, but who has ever suggested that it is a quintessentially American value? On the contrary, nearly every observer has agreed that what marks the American culture is precisely a lack of regimentation, an openness to challenge, spontaneity, even unruliness.

By way of seeing whether negative characterizations of blacks are tied to either of these two sets of values, we shall examine first the relation between aspects of individualism and the perception of blacks as failing to make an effort, and then the relation between these same perceptions of blacks and measures of authoritarian values.

The notion of individualism can be construed in a manifold of ways. Rather than declaring by fiat that only one of these interpretations is the true and central meaning, and the others all parasitic on it, we have instead worked to capture a number of different ways that the notion of individualism is frequently construed. To begin with, individualism surely finds expression in the idea of achievement as a value. Achievement can itself be variously construed, to be sure; but here we shall take it to refer to a person's commitment to excelling, to being the best at what he or she does. Individualism can also convey a special commitment to the idea of success, particularly material success; so one indicator we shall take of the place of individualism in a person's thinking is the importance he or she attaches to making a lot of money. Furthermore, and on a quite different plane, individualism is said to find expression in the striving of one person against others; so we shall take as yet another indicator of individualism the extent to which a person attaches a special measure of importance to competition. For that matter, individualism often carries with it a presumption of the place of self in society, a priority of the claims that one chooses to make on or in behalf of oneself, as against those that others make upon one to fit in, to conform, to follow the approved path. So we shall take as additional indicators of individualism the importance that people attach to their own judgments (as opposed to those of others) as to what they should do, plus the importance they assign to encouraging originality in ideas.

If the perception of blacks as failing to work hard is premised on individualism as a value—as the new racism researchers insist—then some or all of these indicators of individualism will have a marked association with a readiness to perceive blacks as failing to make an effort. But as the chart on page 60 makes plain, virtually *no* relation exists between characterizing blacks as failing to work hard and believing in the idea of individualism—however the idea of individualism is construed.

But what then should be done with the quite common observation made about blacks that they do not work as hard as they could

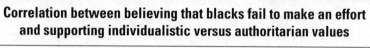

Correlation between believing that blacks fail to make an effort and supporting individualistic versus authoritarian values

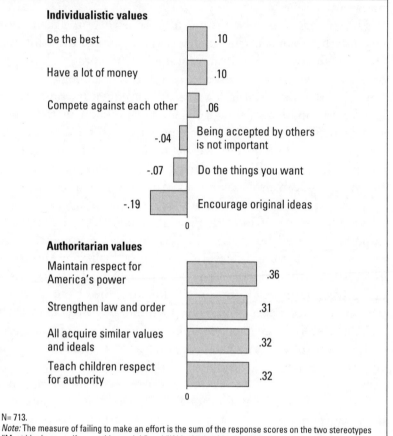

Individualistic values

Be the best	.10
Have a lot of money	.10
Compete against each other	.06
Being accepted by others is not important	-.04
Do the things you want	-.07
Encourage original ideas	-.19

Authoritarian values

Maintain respect for America's power	.36
Strengthen law and order	.31
All acquire similar values and ideals	.32
Teach children respect for authority	.32

N= 713.
Note: The measure of failing to make an effort is the sum of the response scores on the two stereotypes "Most blacks on welfare could get a job" and "If blacks would only try harder, they would be just as well off as whites."

or should? Isn't this, by itself, proof that blacks are rejected because they are perceived to violate the ethic of self-reliance and hard work?

Not at all. Why suppose—as the new racism researchers do—that the person who complains that blacks do not work hard himself works hard? It is foolish to take people's criticism at face value—foolish for more than one reason, but not the least is that it pays to maintain a decent respect for hypocrisy in social affairs. Who would, in our age, automatically believe that the person who repeatedly complains that others are preoccupied with sex is himself indifferent to it? Why, then, uncritically suppose that the person who complains that blacks complain too much does not himself complain too much? Merely because a person believes that blacks are not working as hard as they could or should does not mean that he attaches great importance to hard work or achievement in his own life. Nor does it mean that he is willing to undergo the rigors of competition himself, let alone to steer by his own lights without regard to the opinion of others. In fact, as we have seen, individualism is not relevant one way or the other to perceptions of blacks.

But the case is quite different for authoritarian values. An enormous body of research has demonstrated that people who attach an uncommon importance to obedience and discipline tend to be harsh and judgmental, to be relatively unempathetic and ungenerous, particularly in responding to others who are unfamiliar to them or different in background or belief or appear to deviate from conventional standards of morality and propriety. And it is not difficult to see how, in consequence, people who place an uncommon value on authoritarian values would be more likely to respond to blacks in a way that is more uncharitable, punitive, and judgmental, and hence more likely to perceive blacks as manifesting a number of negative characteristics, among them a lack of discipline, self-control, and willingness to work hard.

And this is exactly what our study confirms. When we asked the following question:

> Given the way things are these days, how important is it to strengthen law and order? Is it very important, somewhat important, or not important?

we found a marked relation between the importance people attach to authority as a value and acceptance of the stereotypes of blacks as failing to make an effort. And as the chart on page 60 also shows, the importance of people's orientations to authority emerges in other measures. For example, everyone was asked if they basically agree (or basically disagree) that:

> Respect for authority is one of the most important things that children should learn.

Again, we found a sizeable tendency for those who place a premium on authority in socialization to accept images of blacks as lazy and irresponsible. Moreover, the value placed on order and authority should be seen, as Adorno and his colleagues urged, as an aspect of a larger outlook, an outlook which emphasizes, among other things, the ideal of conformity, of members of a society subscribing to one common set of values and practices. Accordingly, respondents were asked if they basically agree (or disagree) that:

> The sooner we all acquire similar values and ideals, the better off we'll be.

Agreement with this statement is also substantially correlated with a perception of blacks as failing to try hard.

Finally, it is worth noting one more aspect of the syndrome of authoritarian values. This last aspect points to the emphasis on toughness and domination characteristic of those who attach particular importance to authority as a value. So we asked:

> Now, thinking of the country as a whole, how important is it to maintain respect for America's power in the world, even if that means spending a lot of money on the military? Would you say that is very important, somewhat important, or not important?

Again, as the chart on page 60 shows, the results are perfectly consistent: the more importance a person attaches to maintaining respect for America's power in the world, the more likely he or she is to perceive blacks as failing to make a genuine effort to work hard and to make it on their own.

We want now to turn from the attitudes of whites toward blacks to their attitudes toward policies dealing with blacks, in order to see if in the realm of public policy as well as in the realm of racial stereotypes the force at work is not individualistic values but authoritarian ones. As a representation of racial policy preferences we shall focus on a pair of issues—more government spending in behalf of blacks (see the chart on page 63), and government efforts to ensure fair treatment in employment for blacks (see the chart on page 64). The relation between these policy preferences and the values associated with individualism is very small—indeed, as a rule, indistinguishable from zero. On the other hand, the re-

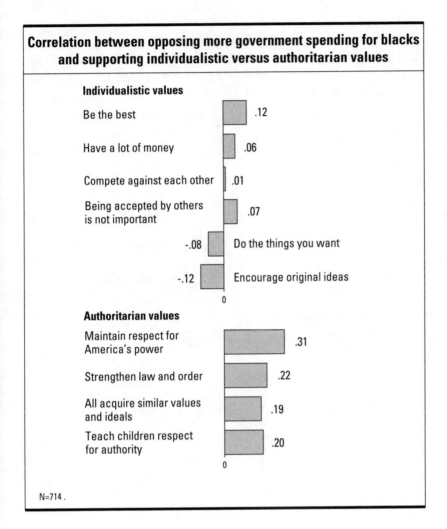

Correlation between opposing more government spending for blacks and supporting individualistic versus authoritarian values

Individualistic values

Be the best .12

Have a lot of money .06

Compete against each other .01

Being accepted by others is not important .07

-.08 Do the things you want

-.12 Encourage original ideas

0

Authoritarian values

Maintain respect for America's power .31

Strengthen law and order .22

All acquire similar values and ideals .19

Teach children respect for authority .20

0

N=714.

lation between opposition to government help for blacks on both policy issues and authoritarian values is similar to what we observed with negative stereotypes of blacks, although weaker in strength.

In short, over a wide range of different conceptions of individualism, and regardless of whether the focus is on white attitudes toward blacks or on white attitudes toward public policies dealing with blacks, the suggestion that the classic American value of individualism is at the heart of the contemporary problem of race is simply, and flatly, wrong.

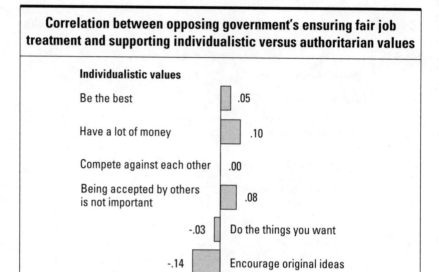

Correlation between opposing government's ensuring fair job treatment and supporting individualistic versus authoritarian values

Individualistic values

Be the best — .05

Have a lot of money — .10

Compete against each other — .00

Being accepted by others is not important — .08

-.03 — Do the things you want

-.14 — Encourage original ideas

Authoritarian values

Maintain respect for America's power — .27

Strengthen law and order — .16

All acquire similar values and ideals — .13

Teach children respect for authority — .17

N= 732.

THE OLD RACISM OR NEW?

By way of summary, four points merit emphasis. First, substantial numbers of Americans are perfectly willing to express frankly negative characterizations of blacks, particularly as failing to try as hard as they could or should to overcome their problems. Second, although racial stereotyping is more common in some parts of American society than in others (showing up more often, for example, among the poorly educated than among the well educated), it is nonetheless widely diffused, and indeed far from uncommon except in pockets of American society that are themselves relatively uncommon by virtue of having both a liberal orientation and an educational advantage. Third, negatively stereotyping blacks is part of a larger syndrome of negatively stereotyping outgroups in general now as before, suggesting that the nature of racism today is the same at its core as it was a generation ago. And fourth, racial stereotyping has very little to do with individualistic values but is instead closely tied up with authoritarian values.

Now, we turn to perhaps the most controversial aspect of contemporary discussions of race—the assertion that modern racism, rather than losing ground, has gone underground. We will show that much of the current discussion of covert racism is misleading—indeed, doubly misleading, giving the impression that racial double standards have taken hold where they have not, while underestimating the strength of racial double standards precisely where they remain strongest.

3

COVERT RACISM AND
DOUBLE STANDARDS

The charge of covert racism has become commonplace. People who oppose affirmative action are, for that reason alone, said to be racists, and people who oppose labeling others as racist on grounds like these are, for that reason alone, said to be racists themselves. The odiousness of the accusation, plus its vagueness, has had a chilling effect on intellectual discussion of the place of race in American life. Ironically, however, the very willingness to announce that racism—in its covert, disguised form—is oppressive everywhere in American life has encouraged the counter-belief that in reality it no longer exists in any significant degree anywhere. The over-readiness to make blanket charges of racism—against people, points of view, institutions—has had an effect very nearly the opposite of the one intended. How seriously can one take the idea of racism if everyone is said to be a racist?

The suggestion that there is a new racism—a racism that has new strength precisely because it doesn't appear to be racism—deserves serious consideration. If true, it shows that an irrational animus against blacks remains more pervasive than many have been willing to acknowledge. If false, it teaches the no less valu-able lesson that a sensitivity to racism, commendable in itself, can have pernicious consequences. Pernicious twice over. To label American values and institutions as racist—when they are *not*—impeaches the very values and institutions that can help overcome racism. And seeing racism where it is not has hidden where it *is*.

Our aim is to explore the extent to which, and the conditions under which, ordinary Americans practice a double standard in determining who is entitled to a public benefit or government service. If asked in the abstract, most Americans would agree that it is wrong for the government to offer assistance to white Americans and then deny exactly the same help to black Americans. But we shall demonstrate that nonetheless a significant number of whites still enforce a racial double standard. In an era in which allegations of racism have become so indiscriminate and self-serving, it is important, we believe, to demonstrate that clear-cut violations of common standards of fair play persist. How many whites will deny a public benefit or service to a black that they would award to a white? When are they most likely to do so? And where in contemporary American society is the practice of racial double standards most common? These are questions that can, for the first time, be answered.

No less important, a focus on racial double standards allows us to come to grips with a fundamental paradox of race in contemporary American life. On the one hand, historic improvements have occurred. Jim Crow has become a phrase of the past, unknown—indeed, very nearly unintelligible—to most Americans under thirty. And unprecedented opportunities for blacks have opened up. A generation ago, it was the highest ambition of civil rights activists that the state be neutral on race—that it stop using its power to impose inequality on blacks; no one suspected it would exert its authority, only a few years later, to see that blacks are preferred to whites. On the other hand, the problem of race manifestly persists, not just in the sense that many blacks are immiserated, though this is surely true, but also in the sense that blacks continue to be penalized by a double standard. By way of partly resolving this paradox of progress and stasis, we shall show that there are two different realities. On the one hand, confronted with an individual who is black, whites are as likely to support the claim of an *individual* black to government assistance as that of a white—indeed, in some circumstances more likely to do so. On the other hand, confronted with blacks *as a group*, a significant number of whites practice a racial double standard. Given this duality of response, it is easier to understand why whites see themselves as living in a world where the meaning of race has changed, while blacks see themselves as living in a world where its meaning has remained much the same.

COVERT RACISM AND TRADITIONAL AMERICAN VALUES

For some time now commentators on public affairs have spoken of a covert racism—a racism that is disguised and subtle but real all the same. Sometimes the notion of covert racism represents no more than an effort to square what seems to be a circle: all the systematic evidence of declining bigotry notwithstanding, race obviously remains a problem in American public life, and—it therefore seems to follow—racism must still persist, albeit under the surface. But the notion of a covert racism has also been developed by the new racism researchers as a part of their self-conscious critique of mainstream American values. According to their central thesis, the overt expression of racial prejudice is now frowned upon. People therefore favor disguised, indirect ways to express their bigotry. They will not say they are opposed to blacks getting help from government because they are black; they will instead say that blacks are not trying to help themselves—and because they are not making a genuine effort on their own, they do not deserve help from others. The perception that blacks "violate cherished values," particularly the values of hard work and individual initiative, has been the spur to a new kind of racism. This new racism, by expressing itself symbolically as support for traditional American values, can disguise itself. Ironically, then, what is *new* about the new racism is its expropriation of traditional values as a cloak to hide its true nature, which consists of prejudice and bigotry.

In the last chapter we saw that, in fact, people who highly value individualism are not especially prone to accept negative stereotypes about blacks, including stereotypes of blacks as failing to work hard and to stand on their own two feet. We want to turn now from what whites *say* about blacks to how they *treat* them—and in particular whether they are willing to treat them the same as whites. We will report the results of the first experiments carried out in a public opinion survey to detect covert racism—to determine scientifically if blacks are penalized because they are black and, still more specifically, to determine the extent to which individualism and other mainstream values in fact encourage a racial double standard in judging who is and is not entitled to government assistance.

THE "LAID-OFF WORKER" EXPERIMENT

We rarely encounter the issue of race in the abstract. People find themselves on a street late at night, walking to their car, when they spot on the other side of the street male teenagers: What difference does it make if the teenagers are black? Alternatively, a person may be sitting across the desk from an applicant for a job, who has done reasonably well in school apart from a problem in attendance: What difference does it make if the applicant is black rather than white? Exactly this kind of question, applied to politics, is what we want to address. Individuals routinely make claims for a public benefit or a governmental service—for assistance in finding work, for support in obtaining a better education, for a permit authorizing a business, for an indefinite number and variety of public services—and what needs to be determined is what difference it makes to white Americans if the person requesting a particular benefit or service is black.

Whites may no longer single out a black with a PhD for rebuff, but how will they react if they have a potentially legitimate basis available to them to reject the black's claim? Suppose he has lost his job and wants assistance in finding another, but it turns out that he has not been a very dependable worker? Can they not take advantage of this blemish on his work record and, pointing to it, reject his request for assistance without having to worry about appearing racist? Or, to take a situation which supplies a similarly plausible, nonprejudiced explanation for what might be considered prejudiced behavior, suppose a black woman fails to uphold traditional family values—let's say she's a single mother. Will whites take advantage of this pretext to reject her request for government assistance?

The whole point of the covert racism idea is the claim that substantial numbers of whites, given a socially acceptable pretext, will take advantage of it and express the spite, resentment, and hostility they feel toward blacks. Ideally, then, we need to create a situation in which two people, exactly alike in every respect except for race, make a request for government assistance, and see if the request of the white is approved and that of the black is denied. And what is more, we want to accomplish this without tipping off respondents about what we're up to. The laid-off worker experiment was designed specifically to accomplish this. The basic rationale behind the experiment is this: Respondents are asked to decide whether a person who has lost his or her job is entitled to government assistance in finding another one. Some of the characteristics of the person laid off are described in the process, including whether the laid-off worker is black or white. All this is deliberately done in a way to create different circumstances which can legitimize a negative reaction to blacks. In particular, three distinct combinations of characteristics—the "lazy" black, the black who violates traditional family values, and the young, male black—were created to legitimize a negative reaction to blacks. In each case, by experimentally randomizing the characteristics of the laid-off worker, it can be authoritatively determined whether whites respond more negatively to a black—without their being in a position to know that this analysis is going on.

The laid-off worker experiment begins with an introduction announcing that the next question concerns a person "laid off because the company where he or she worked had to reduce its staff." The interviewer asks respondents to "think for a moment about the person and then tell me how much government help, if any, that person should receive while looking for a new job," and then describes the laid-off worker. Specifically, the interviewer says:

> The first person is a [WHITE or a BLACK] [MALE or FEMALE], in [HIS or HER] [EARLY TWENTIES, MID-THIRTIES, or EARLY FORTIES]. HE/SHE is [SINGLE, A SINGLE PARENT, MARRIED, MARRIED AND HAS CHILDREN] and [IS A DEPENDABLE WORKER or IS NOT A VERY DEPENDABLE WORKER].

The description of the laid-off worker is determined by computer-generated random numbers, with the value of each characteristic independently determined. The experiment is thus designed to assess the impact of a variety of personal characteristics of the laid-off worker—for example, whether the person is white or black, single or has a family—on the amount of help the person is judged to be entitled to receive from the government in finding a new job, and in addition, the impact of each combination of these characteristics. Judgments about whether the person who has lost his or her job should receive government help are scored 0 for "none at all," 5 for "some," and 10 for "a lot," so in the analysis that follows, the higher the score, the more positive (or in favor of assistance) the response.

The design of the laid-off worker experiment is quite complex. The traditional public opinion survey may ask a few special questions in two forms, one addressed to one half of the sample, the other to the other half. The laid-off worker experiment, in contrast, involves 96 different combinations. And thanks precisely to the variety of forms the experiment assumes, it allows us to investigate in a way never before possible the problem of covert racism. Through strategic, deliberately contrived, and experimentally manipulated presentation, blacks are presented as violating traditional American values, either by failing to keep the nuclear family intact or by failing to work hard. The laid-off worker experiment thus deliberately presents some respondents with a situation in which they are free to respond negatively to a black, since the black has violated a consensual value; and because of the power of experimental randomization, the extent to which whites take advantage of an opportunity to respond negatively to blacks without the risk of appearing to be racist can be measured effectively and without bias.

Although the experiment's design is complex, its administration is quite simple. The selection of the values of the personal characteristics of the laid-off worker is determined by a computer. The interviewer needs only to read a question, of standard length and complexity, which appears automatically on his or her computer screen, then record the respondent's choice of a response category, again from a standard set of response categories. The experiment is thus effortless to conduct from the point of view of the interviewer, all the manipulations being done by a computer, and invisible from the point of view of the respondent, with no cues supplied that it is all part of a complex effort to assess covert racism. Indeed, from both the respondent's and the interviewer's points of view, the question about the laid-off worker does not appear to be an experiment at all, just one more item in an ordinary interview.

Who is more inclined to use a double standard in the laid-off worker experiment, a white conservative or a white liberal? The warnings about the new racism concentrate on the danger from the political right, and it is not hard to understand why. Almost by definition, a conservative is more likely than a liberal to oppose efforts to increase government spending to assist blacks, for example; indeed, is more likely to oppose a range of public policies designed to help blacks. But does it follow that the conservative is racist?

Not necessarily. His opposition to activist government may be inspired not by racism but by conservatism itself. A conservative, in the nature of things, should manifestly be more likely than a liberal to attend to the risks and the costs of bigger government bureaucracies and the like. It is simply unreasonable to insist that a conservative be as enthusiastic as a liberal about government spending for social programs or else stand convicted of being a racist.

The test of whether conservatism is now joined to racism is whether the conservative treats all claimants for government assistance alike: insofar as conservatives judge that a white is entitled to government help but a black, identically situated and making the identical claim, is not, then conservatives are racist.

By way of locating a standard of comparison, let us first consider whether people who have described themselves as liberals penalize blacks—and black males in particular—by applying a racial double standard. This is not an idle exercise. Everybody is suspected by somebody of being a racist nowadays, and liberals are not exempt from suspicion if only because of the ambivalence toward blacks they are alleged to harbor. What we found, to the contrary, is that the race of the potential beneficiary makes no difference to white liberals. On the other hand, our results suggest that the *gender* of the laid-off worker can make a difference to liberals. The mean score for government assistance when the laid-off worker is a woman is 5.8, compared with 4.8 when the person losing a job is a man. Closer examination of the results, however, makes plain what is going on. As the chart on page 73 shows, liberals are distinctly less sympathetic to the claims of white men compared with their response to women, especially to white women.

Now, let us consider the reactions of people who have described themselves as conservatives to a claim for government assistance on behalf of a person who has lost his job. The covert racism thesis predicts that conservatives will respond more negatively to a black

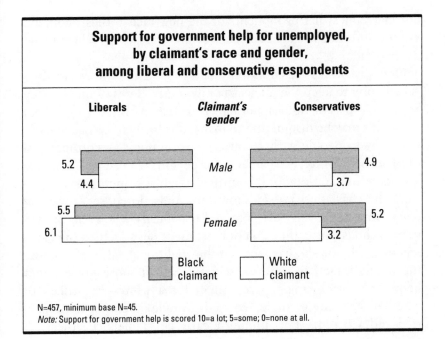

**Support for government help for unemployed,
by claimant's race and gender,
among liberal and conservative respondents**

Liberals	*Claimant's gender*	Conservatives
5.2 / 4.4	*Male*	4.9 / 3.7
5.5 / 6.1	*Female*	5.2 / 3.2

■ Black claimant   □ White claimant

N=457, minimum base N=45.
Note: Support for government help is scored 10=a lot; 5=some; 0=none at all.

than to a white. We found that the race of the potential beneficiary does make a difference to conservatives, but in exactly the opposite way from what the thesis predicts. Conservatives are more likely to favor government help for a black than for a white.

The gender of the potential beneficiary makes no difference to conservatives, and conservatives do not react more negatively to the claims of black males. On the contrary, they are more likely to support government assistance for a black male than for either a white male or a white female.

These findings are surely counterintuitive. Not only do conservatives not react as the covert racism thesis predicts they will react; they react in the very opposite way—favoring blacks rather than discriminating against them. But perhaps the test is too crude; perhaps it is necessary to take account of a more subtle form of racism. Conservatives may not feel free to react against blacks in all circumstances, but they may disclose a hidden animus if they are supplied with a pretext to legitimize a negative reaction. Suppose, then, that we supplied a person of conservative outlook with exactly the sort of stereotypical symbol of blacks' violation of traditional values that proponents of the new racism thesis contend excites and cloaks negative feelings about blacks? What would happen then?

One way blacks are commonly said to violate traditional values is by failing to keep the nuclear family intact. Rates of illegitimacy and single parent homes among blacks are alarmingly high, and while this may be disquieting to many, it is likely to be particularly vexatious to people with a conservative outlook. Accordingly, in the laid-off worker experiment the person in need of assistance was sometimes (at random) identified as a black single parent.

As the chart on page 75 shows, not only do conservatives *not* react more negatively to a potential beneficiary who is black than to one who is white, they do not react more negatively to the black *even* when he or she has violated the traditional value of keeping the family intact. Indeed, conservatives favor more government help for a black single parent than for a white—regardless of whether the white is single, married, a single parent, or both married and a parent. This finding clearly contradicts the thesis of covert racism: conservatives do not take advantage of the pretext supplied them to vent their negative feelings about blacks. The covert racism thesis thus misses the mark twice over. Conservatives do not treat a claim for government assistance by a black worse than one by a white; and insofar as they do take account of the race of a potential beneficiary, it is to respond more positively, not more negatively, to blacks.

But why are conservatives more likely to favor government assistance for a black claimant than for a white one? One hint at what is going on comes from classic studies showing that responses to blacks are highly contingent on "social responsibility" cues. In one experiment, for example, subjects were presented with a picture of a black male, then asked to describe his personal characteristics. In one condition of the experiment, the man in the photograph wore a t-shirt; in the other, a tie. Wearing a t-shirt, the black was perceived to be lazy, undependable, unintelligent; wearing a tie, the very same person was perceived to be industrious, reliable, intelligent. With this classic study in mind, we designed the laid-off worker experiment to manipulate the work history of the claimant. In one condition, the claimant is described as a dependable worker; in the other, as an undependable worker.

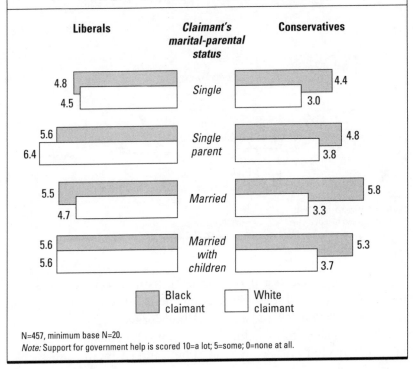

**Support for government help for unemployed,
by claimant's race and marital-parental status,
among liberal and conservative respondents**

Liberals	Claimant's marital-parental status	Conservatives

Liberals — Single: 4.8 (Black), 4.5 (White)
Conservatives — Single: 4.4 (Black), 3.0 (White)

Liberals — Single parent: 5.6 (Black), 6.4 (White)
Conservatives — Single parent: 4.8 (Black), 3.8 (White)

Liberals — Married: 5.5 (Black), 4.7 (White)
Conservatives — Married: 5.8 (Black), 3.3 (White)

Liberals — Married with children: 5.6 (Black), 5.6 (White)
Conservatives — Married with children: 5.3 (Black), 3.7 (White)

Black claimant / White claimant

N=457, minimum base N=20.
Note: Support for government help is scored 10=a lot; 5=some; 0=none at all.

Looking first at liberals, we found that neither the race nor the work history of the claimant is regarded as a relevant consideration in judging whether the government should assist a person who has been laid off in finding a new job. As the chart on page 76 shows, it makes virtually no difference to liberals whether the person who has lost his or her job is black or white, or has been a dependable worker or an undependable worker, in making a judgment whether the claimant is entitled to assistance from the government in finding a new job.

Looking next at conservatives, we can see that they are, as we would expect, in general cool to the idea of government assistance. They are manifestly not in favor when the person who has lost his job has not been a hard worker, whether white or black. Nor are they in favor of government assistance even in the case of a white

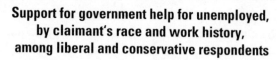

Support for government help for unemployed, by claimant's race and work history, among liberal and conservative respondents

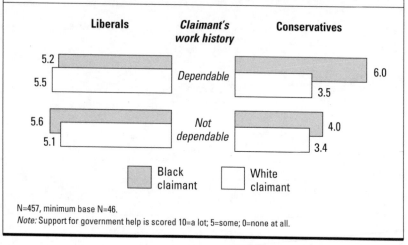

	Liberals	Claimant's work history	Conservatives
	5.2 / 5.5	Dependable	6.0 / 3.5
	5.6 / 5.1	Not dependable	4.0 / 3.4

Black claimant / White claimant

N=457, minimum base N=46.
Note: Support for government help is scored 10=a lot; 5=some; 0=none at all.

person who has been a hard worker. But they come down strikingly in favor of a lot of government help if the person who has lost a job is *both* black and a dependable worker.

What we need to explain, then, is not why conservatives react more positively to blacks in general but rather why they deviate so markedly from their conservative outlook in the particular case of a black who has been a dependable employee. As we shall show in Chapter 5, conservatives are more likely than liberals to believe that blacks are not trying as hard as they could or should, more likely, that is, to see a hard-working black as an exception. "This one," they say to themselves, "is not like the others; this one is really trying." And perceiving *this* black to be an exception—perceiving him to be a person who exemplifies the values of individual effort and striving they admire—they make an exception. Thus, precisely because they think less of blacks as a group, conservatives paradoxically can wind up wanting to do more for them as individuals.

People with a conservative outlook do tend to reject the idea that an undependable black deserves to get a lot of government help in finding a new job. But of course, being conservative, they are naturally inclined to oppose government help of this kind, whoever will get it. They do not single blacks out. In fact, they are, if anything, more opposed to a white getting this help, whether a dependable worker or an undependable one.

It may be objected that the results of the laid-off worker experiment are artifactual. Telling respondents that a laid-off worker is black may tip them off to the purpose of the experiment: hearing this, the more biased among them may give a more positive response than they otherwise would, precisely in order to cover up their negative feelings toward blacks. It is always possible to imagine a person has doped out the intent of an experiment and "faked good." But this particular objection fails on logical grounds. It asserts that respondents, hearing the person out of work described as black and suspecting that they may appear racist if they opposed government assistance for the laid-off worker, therefore supported it. But if this is correct, then there should be more support for government assistance for the black laid-off worker across-the-board: whites wanting to forestall an imputation of racism should be more likely to favor government help for a black who was undependable than for a white who was undependable, and ditto for a black and a white both of whom were dependable. Yet, the difference shows up only for a black who is a dependable worker. As we saw, there is no significant difference in their willingness to favor government help for a black than for a white if both were undependable—*indeed, no more willingness to favor help for a dependable white than for an undependable black.* There is more support for assistance for a laid-off worker who is black if, and only if, the claimant is *both* black and a dependable worker.

A second objection could be made, however. Respondents are told whether a black is, or is not, dependable. But in real life, isn't the risk precisely that a judgment about an individual will be made on the basis not of his or her actual qualities but rather by virtue of stereotypes attributed on the basis of race? Seeing a person is black, won't conservatives tend to perceive him as undependable? They might not discriminate against a black if they know that he is a hard worker; but the whole point, a thoughtful critic may say, is that conservatives are predisposed to believe that a black is *not* a hard worker.

This second objection is more plausible than the first, but just as wrong. Conservatives encounter, in one condition of the laid-off worker experiment, an undependable black. This black is actually described as—not merely inferred to be—undependable. A crucial comparison, then, is how conservatives react to an undependable black, as compared with a dependable white: that is, after all, precisely the comparison which maximizes their legitimate opportunity to respond negatively to blacks. But there is no significant difference in the way that conservatives treat the two: they are opposed to the government's helping a hard-working white find a new job just as they are opposed to the government's assisting an undependable black. Which is as it should be: from the perspective of a conservative, the point is to resist expansion of government activism. This is a principle they subscribe to and consistently support, making an exception to it only when they confront what is (from their point of view) itself an exception—a hard-working black.

Given all the loose talk about covert racism, it is important to speak plainly about our results in the laid-off worker experiment. We deliberately waved a red flag, focusing on a black who had lost his job, specifically described as undependable on the job, and who nonetheless wanted government assistance. Yet conservatives, supplied with an ideal pretext to justify a negative reaction to blacks, did not exploit it. In short, the absence of an especially negative reaction to blacks, even when a pretext for one is supplied, is a striking example of the "Sherlock Holmes dog that did not bark"—a result that is striking not because of what did happen but because of what did not.

THE "EQUAL OPPORTUNITY" EXPERIMENT

The laid-off worker experiment shows that a racial double standard is *not* applied by whites in judging whether a person who has lost a job should receive assistance from the government in finding another. But should the absence of a racial double standard in judgments of this type be taken as proof of the absence of racial discrimination more broadly?

Consider the logic of the laid-off worker experiment. It is not blacks in general that a person is asked to respond to but a particular person, one who, in addition to being black, has a specific work history, background, and distinguishing characteristics. The design of the laid-off worker experiment thus focuses attention on the individuating characteristics of a specific person, which is precisely the opposite of a situation which facilitates a stereotypical response. In contrast, consider the kind of judgments that citizens more often are asked to make about politics and race. Should government spending be increased to improve the social and economic position of blacks? Should an antidiscrimination law in housing be passed? Should admissions to colleges and universities be made partly on the basis of the applicant's race? All these are judgments not about what should be done for a specific person who happens to be black but for blacks as a group. And because people are being asked to respond, on an immediate basis and without an extended opportunity for deliberation, to blacks taken as a group, their responses are more likely to be driven by stereotypes about blacks as a group. Thus, it is easy to argue that, notwithstanding the results of the laid-off worker experiment, since conservatives are more likely to hold negative stereotypes of blacks than are liberals, conservatives may discriminate against blacks at the level of policy even if they do not discriminate against them as individuals.

The equal opportunity experiment was performed to test this hypothesis. The basic idea is to focus on a policy effort which could plausibly be made in behalf of several different groups, one of which is blacks, and then see if whites are more willing to support exactly the same program if the beneficiary is a group other than blacks. Suppose there are two groups, one of which is blacks, either of which can plausibly lay claim to a particular public benefit or governmental service. Suppose further that the second group could not plausibly make a more compelling claim than blacks to the particular benefit or service, though it could conceivably make as strong a claim. In these circumstances, we shall define as a racial double standard a significantly greater willingness to affirm that the nonblack group is entitled to the governmental benefit or service than the black group.

We focused on the government's obligation to assure equal opportunity to succeed. Respondents were not asked to support equal outcomes, only to approve of government efforts to assure equal opportunities to succeed. The two groups compared were "blacks" and "women," the pair having been chosen to assure an asymmetry in standing: it is often argued that government is under a special obligation to assist blacks, that the burden of slavery and discrimination that blacks have borne in America is a uniquely oppressive burden. It is occasionally argued that the needs of women approach those of blacks, but it is not explicitly argued by anyone that the oppression of women eclipses that of blacks, and hence that the government should work to achieve equal opportunity for women—but that it ought not to do so for blacks. We shall, accordingly, interpret more support for government intervention to assure equal opportunity for women than for blacks as evidence of a double standard.

The equal opportunity experiment thus consists in experimentally contrasting reactions to two versions of otherwise identical questions. In one version, the statement is worded:

> While equal opportunity for blacks and minorities to succeed is important, it's not really the government's job to guarantee it.

In the other version, the statement is exactly the same in all respects except one: instead of referring to blacks and minorities, it refers to women.

Consider first the responses of conservatives. As the chart on page 81 shows, they are significantly more likely to favor help for women than for blacks: 45 percent of them support government guarantees of equal opportunity for women, as compared with only 28 percent for blacks. Self-identified conservatives, the results of the equal opportunity experiment demonstrate, *do* practice a racial double standard in judging the claims of groups, if not those of individuals. But so do self-identified liberals: 69 percent of them believe that government should guarantee equal opportunity for women, as compared with only 54 percent for blacks.

The outcome of the equal opportunity experiment is thus the opposite of the laid-off worker experiment. When whites react not to individual blacks but to blacks as a group, a double standard is plain, and it shows up not in one particular narrow segment but across the political spectrum. Liberals are just as likely to discriminate as conservatives. An innocent explanation of the greater support for government guarantees of equal opportunity for women than for blacks could be the greater responsiveness of women, whether liberal or conservative, to an appeal to improve the

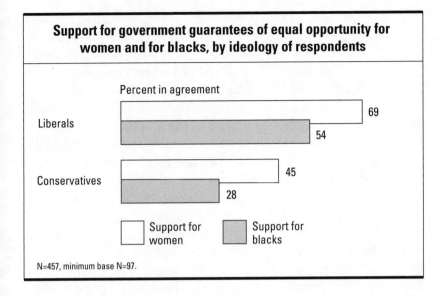

Support for government guarantees of equal opportunity for women and for blacks, by ideology of respondents

Percent in agreement

Liberals
69
54

Conservatives
45
28

☐ Support for women   ▨ Support for blacks

N=457, minimum base N=97.

opportunities open to them. But in fact, the reactions of women and men on this issue do not differ significantly.

Proponents of the covert racism thesis most often see the danger to be predominantly on the right, but some have warned of hazards of racism on the left. For our part, this stress on ideology as a source of racism, whether oriented to the left or the right, misses the point. As the classic studies of prejudice from a generation ago drove home, intolerance is strongest precisely in those parts of society where the power of abstract ideas is weakest, that is, among those with little formal education. On the one side, the less schooling people have had, the more likely they are to exhibit the simplistic thinking, plus the diffuse anger and apprehension, that favor intolerance. On the other side, the more schooling they have had, the more likely are the larger ideas of politics, on the left or on the right, to come alive for them and guide their political judgments.

Suppose the public is divided up, with those best equipped to understand political ideas of the left or of the right put in one pile, and those least equipped to do so in another. We would expect that those equipped by virtue of education to understand the political point of view they profess would make their choices in conformity with it, while those less prepared to grasp the implications of their orientations would be the most likely to have their judgment of what should be done determined not by any larger conception of how government should act but rather on the basis of who is to benefit from government action—blacks or nonblacks.

Consider first well-educated whites. Well-educated liberals should favor government assurance of equal opportunity; and certainly if they understand what liberalism is about, it should be irrelevant whether the beneficiaries are to be blacks or women: in either case, from a liberal perspective, it is the business of government actively to assure equal opportunity for those who historically have been disadvantaged. Equivalently but inversely, well-educated conservatives should oppose such proposals for government activism, and they should oppose them as much if government intervention is proposed in the service of women as in the service of blacks. The issue, from a conservative point of view, is not *who* is to benefit from interventionist social policies but rather whether government ought to intervene in this way in anybody's behalf.

And indeed we found that it makes no significant difference to well-educated liberals if a claim is made in behalf of blacks or of women: as liberals, they favor the idea of a more activist government, and they accordingly are just as likely to believe that the government should guarantee equal opportunity to succeed for blacks as for women. And the position is exactly the same, except the other way around, for well-educated conservatives. As the chart on page 83 makes plain, it makes no significant difference whatever to them if a claim is made in behalf of blacks or of women: as conservatives, they are just as likely to believe that it is no business of the government in either case.

But if the well-educated are even-handed in their judgments, both on the left or the right, those with a high school education or less manifestly practice a racial double standard whether they are on the left or the right. Thus, conservatives with a high school education or less are almost three times as likely to approve of government assurances of equal opportunity for women as for blacks—plainly a double standard. But the situation is the same on the left. Self-identified liberals at the same educational level are

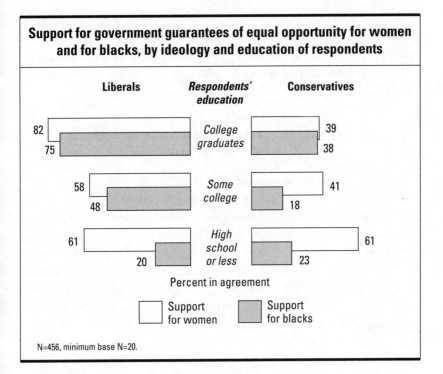

Support for government guarantees of equal opportunity for women and for blacks, by ideology and education of respondents

Liberals — Respondents' education — Conservatives

College graduates: Liberals 82 (women), 75 (blacks); Conservatives 39 (women), 38 (blacks)

Some college: Liberals 58 (women), 48 (blacks); Conservatives 41 (women), 18 (blacks)

High school or less: Liberals 61 (women), 20 (blacks); Conservatives 61 (women), 23 (blacks)

Percent in agreement

Support for women · Support for blacks

N=456, minimum base N=20.

also three times as likely to support government intervention for women as for blacks. Education, these results suggest, plays a critical role in combatting racial double standards, and a variety of more specific analyses confirm this.

Since having relatively little formal education tends to go hand in hand with having a relatively low income, it could be argued that the crucial factor behind intolerance is economic adversity, not a lack of formal education. In fact, taking both formal schooling and total family income into account at the same time makes plain that education is the crucial factor. Among well-educated whites, the lower a person's income, the *more* likely he or she is to believe that government ought to assure blacks an equal opportunity to succeed, and indeed those whites who are both relatively poor and also well educated are more likely to favor blacks over women. On the other hand, the less-educated whites, *regardless of their income*, are markedly more likely to judge that the government ought to assure equal opportunity for women than for blacks.

To summarize, contrary to the common notion that racial double standards are rooted in a conservative political ideology, what promotes racial double standards is precisely a lack of exposure to and familiarity with abstract ideas, whether on the left or the right.

MAINSTREAM AMERICAN VALUES AND THE DOUBLE STANDARD

A central theme of the research of the last decade, as we saw in Chapter 2, is that mainstream American values—the ideas and ideals central to the American self-image—are deeply and directly implicated in contemporary racism. Achievement, independence, individuality—all are alleged to have gone into partnership with racism. The thrust of the charge goes deep. It asserts that contemporary racism, rather than reflecting ignorance of American principles, is rooted in the "finest and proudest of traditional American values." So we next want to consider, if only briefly, a wide range of values and concerns, including preserving traditional ideas of right and wrong, individual achievement, competition, adherence to God's will, strengthening law and order, respect for authority, opposition to welfare, opposition to spending on the problems of big cities, and even the importance of maintaining respect for America's power in the world—and see how people who hold these values respond in the laid-off worker and the equal opportunity experiments.

If mainstream American values, in any or all of these incarnations, are implicated in contemporary racism, it ought to be the case that proponents of these ideals will be more likely to practice a racial double standard. But we found the opposite. Although the differences are small, in seven of the nine comparisons they are statistically significant, and every one shows a *more* positive response to a black out of work than to a white, as the chart on page 85 shows. Simply put, whatever the traditional American value considered, the findings not only fail to support the new racism thesis; they are directly at odds with it. Moreover, analyses of the equal opportunity experiment similarly demonstrate that proponents of traditional values do not practice a double standard in judging who is entitled to government assistance.

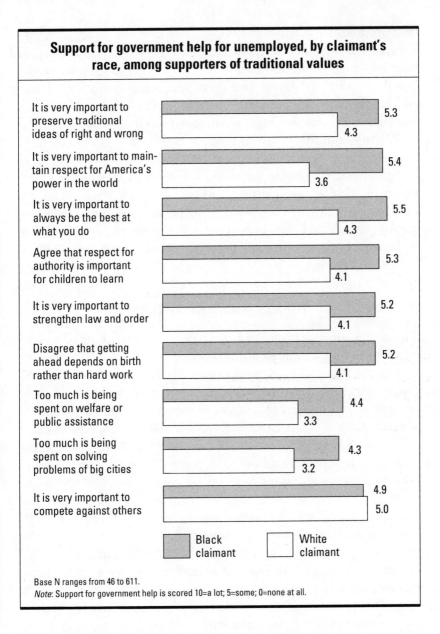

Support for government help for unemployed, by claimant's race, among supporters of traditional values

	Black claimant	White claimant
It is very important to preserve traditional ideas of right and wrong	5.3	4.3
It is very important to maintain respect for America's power in the world	5.4	3.6
It is very important to always be the best at what you do	5.5	4.3
Agree that respect for authority is important for children to learn	5.3	4.1
It is very important to strengthen law and order	5.2	4.1
Disagree that getting ahead depends on birth rather than hard work	5.2	4.1
Too much is being spent on welfare or public assistance	4.4	3.3
Too much is being spent on solving problems of big cities	4.3	3.2
It is very important to compete against others	4.9	5.0

Base N ranges from 46 to 611.
Note: Support for government help is scored 10=a lot; 5=some; 0=none at all.

Nevertheless, we found one instance which seems to support the new racism argument: those who think that preserving traditional ideas of right and wrong are very important are more likely to believe that government should guarantee equal opportunity to succeed for women than for blacks. But if we control for education, we find that it is not the importance that one attaches to traditional morality per se that matters: among the well educated, both those who believe that it is very important to preserve traditional morality and those who do not treat the claims of women and blacks alike. By contrast, among the less educated, there is markedly more support for government assistance for women than for blacks—and this is just as true for those who believe that it is *not* important to preserve traditional values as for those who believe that it is. The importance that a person attaches to traditional values does not matter. It only seems as though there is a link between racism and wanting to preserve traditional values because simplistic values appeal most to the least educated, and it is the least educated who are the most prone to racism, whatever values they profess.

THEMES AND ANTITHEMES

The charge of covert racism is destructive. Accusations of racism have been leveled so often and so recklessly that the public discussion of the place of race in American life has become politicized and deadlocked. Less obviously, the charge of covert racism has become a handmaiden of a larger argument to call into question the principles of American society. A generation ago, scholars and public commentators saw racism as antithetical to the central values of the American ethos. Now, some researchers see contemporary racism as an expression of these very values. Covert racism is alleged to be commonplace, reinforced by quintessentially American values such as self-reliance, individual initiative, the desire to achieve and to excel—above all, the master idea of individualism. Moreover, rather than being concentrated at the margin of American life, racism is now said to have entered the mainstream and to have become, if not ubiquitous, at any rate all too common throughout contemporary American society.

Our findings show this to be wrong, indeed, wrong twice over: by suggesting that racism is strong in parts of American society where it is in fact weak, while giving the impression that it is weak in precisely those parts where it is in fact strong. Racism, as expressed in the application of a double standard, far from being driven by a set of ideas about individualism, is strongest in that part of American society least prepared and accustomed to respond to politics on the basis of any ideas whatsoever, whether about individualism or equality or any other subject. What is more, the fashionable talk of "subtle" racism and the "superficial" tolerance acquired through formal education has helped to conceal the fact—crucial to understanding racism in the 1980s and 90s—that it is precisely the lack of schooling, and everything that goes with this, which most effectively leads to blacks' being penalized merely by virtue of being black. If one wishes to combat racism, then a lack of education, and the ignorance and simplism it abets, is what one must contend against, and it is exactly societal institutions like schools, which encourage subtlety and complexity of thought and expression, which one ought to protect. Seeing racism where it is not and failing to see it where it is, some contemporary commentators on race have tended to ignore what they should criticize, and to criticize what they should defend.

4

PREJUDICE AND
POLITICS

How do whites go about making up their minds whether they favor or oppose increasing the amount of government funding for assistance to blacks, or ensuring that a desired number of blacks are admitted to colleges and universities, or yet again, passing a law against racial discrimination in housing? We want to focus in this chapter on the connection between the feelings whites harbor toward blacks and the positions that they take on issues dealing with blacks—to explore how far white opposition to public policies designed to assist blacks is driven by race prejudice.

A racial bigot is not likely to be a champion of affirmative action—or for that matter of medical care for elderly, central-city residents. But without denying the importance of sheer dislike of blacks as a basis for racial policy preferences, we shall show that the connections between racial stereotypes whites accept about blacks and the positions they take on issues dealing with blacks are both more complex and more troubling than is commonly supposed. More complex because some issues of race are heavily, others only marginally, influenced by racial stereotypes; more troubling because the impact of racial stereotypes on the political thinking of ordinary Americans, so far from being concentrated among those who are patently bigoted, extends broadly into the larger public.

WHICH STEREOTYPES MATTER?

A person may accept a particular negative characterization of a group for any of a number of reasons—because he dislikes the group, because others he relies on have told him the characterization is correct, even because the characterization in fact has a kernel of truth. But if the reasons for accepting any one negative characterization are ambiguous, it is otherwise when a person evinces a *systematic* readiness to endorse negative stereotypes. The more frequently and consistently a person endorses negative characterizations of blacks, the more racially prejudiced that person is—indeed, following standard practice, by prejudice we mean precisely a consistent readiness to respond negatively to a member of a group by virtue of his or her membership in the group, with the proof of prejudice being thus the repetitiveness with which a person endorses negative characterization after negative characterization.

But how does prejudice shape the political thinking of whites? Intuitively, it seems obvious that the more that whites dislike blacks, the more likely they should be to oppose any given policy designed to help blacks. In the figure on page 90, a person's position on the horizontal axis reflects his dislike of blacks; his position on the vertical axis reflects the probability of his opposing a public policy designed to assist blacks. The further to the right a person falls on the horizontal axis, the more negative his feelings toward blacks, and the higher he stands on the vertical axis, the more certain he is to oppose government assistance for blacks.

The solid line in the figure ("Model 1") makes explicit a pair of intuitions underlying the commonsense expectation that whites decide their positions on racial issues as a function of their feelings toward blacks. The more that whites dislike blacks—as measured by the number of negative stereotypes about blacks they endorse—the more likely they are to oppose public policies intended to assist them, a trend captured by the ascent of the solid line as it moves from left to right. But even more important, the

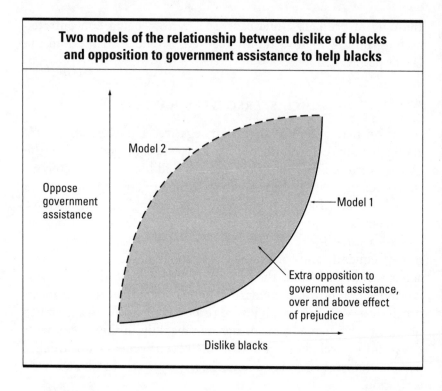

Two models of the relationship between dislike of blacks and opposition to government assistance to help blacks

Oppose government assistance

Model 2

Model 1

Extra opposition to government assistance, over and above effect of prejudice

Dislike blacks

more emphatic or pronounced whites' dislike of blacks, the more likely they are to base their positions on issues of race on their dislike of blacks, and this is captured in the figure by the increasing sharpness of the ascent of the line as it approaches the right side of the horizontal axis. A person who accepts one or even two negative characterizations of blacks is unlikely to base his or her positions on racial issues entirely on this. On the other hand, the person who takes advantage of every opportunity that comes his way to denigrate blacks is likely to have his feelings toward blacks very much in mind when deciding whether the amount of government money spent to help blacks should be increased or not. Hence the slope of the solid line, moving from left to right in the figure, ascends only slightly at first and then rises sharply, indicating the increasingly prominent role of dislike for blacks in shaping political thinking.

The idea that the more that whites dislike blacks, the more likely they are to oppose policies to help blacks, although a commonsensical idea, is a powerful one. If correct, it teaches that particulars on both sides do not count for much—neither the particular stereotype that whites hold nor the particular racial policy put before them. Whatever the objectives a racial policy proposes to accomplish or however it proposes to accomplish them does not matter—the form of the curve should be the same, with whites being more likely to dislike the policy the more they dislike blacks. On the other side, the particular negative characterizations of blacks do not much matter either—what matters is how many of them whites hold.

We would like to sketch a different picture of how whites' images of blacks can affect their thinking about issues of race. The same figure shows a second curve, dotted rather than solid. The dotted curve ("Model 2") describes the probability of opposition to a racial policy like government spending to assist blacks as a function of the acceptance of *particular* negative characterizations of blacks. The dotted and solid lines differ dramatically. Whereas the solid line rises gradually at first and then steeply, the dotted line shoots up quickly and thereafter rises only slightly. The shape of the dotted line is meant to suggest that what matters is not the total number of racial stereotypes that a white harbors, but rather whether he or she accepts one or two particularly crucial negative characterizations of blacks. An example of such a crucial characterization is believing that blacks could be far better off if they worked harder. Believe this, the dotted line suggests, and you will be likely to oppose more government assistance for blacks—and you will be likely to oppose it whether or not you think blacks are more likely to be mixed up in crime than whites, or more pleasure-loving, or whatever.

The bulge in the figure—the large shaded area—indicates the proportion of whites opposing policies to assist blacks *above and beyond those whites who are racially prejudiced.* What we have here is a key to a central paradox of race and American politics. On the one hand, a host of studies testify to the significant decline in the proportion of whites who are out-and-out bigots. On the other hand, it is still strongly suspected that the responses of a large number of whites to at least some issues of race remain strongly influenced by racial stereotypes. The shaded area offers the key to reconciling the two. For it identifies the sizeable part of the public who reject policies to assist blacks not because they are prejudiced—that is, prone consistently to endorse racial stereo-types across-the-board—but because they accept one or possibly two particular negative characterizations in common circulation.

By way of developing this idea, we want to begin by focusing on one of the three racial policy agendas we have identified—the social welfare agenda. How far are the positions that whites take on issues of social welfare driven by race prejudice?

THE SOCIAL WELFARE AGENDA

To begin to answer this question, we created a summary measure of stereotypes by assigning a point to respondents for every nega-tive characterization of blacks they accept: from whether they believe that most blacks tend to have a chip on their shoulder, do not try hard enough, let their neighborhoods run down, take advantage of welfare, tend to be more violent than whites, and are born with less ability. This measure we call the Overall Index of negative racial stereotypes. In addition, we combined their reac-tion to *only two* of the negative characterizations—that blacks could be as well off as whites if they would only work harder and that blacks take advantage of welfare. The basic idea behind this Effort Index is of course that the way to tell whether a person is making a genuine effort to overcome social and economic prob-lems is by looking at his or her willingness to work.

Every component in the Effort Index is included in the Overall Index; and not only are all six of the negative stereotypes highly correlated with every other, but every one of them is also highly correlated with items expressing anti-Semitic stereotypes. An index with more items will be more reliable than one with fewer items; hence, a longer measure will almost always be a better predictor than a short one. We would expect, then, that the six-item Overall Index of negative racial stereotypes would be more highly correlated with the positions of whites on government assistance for blacks than would the two-item Effort Index.

In fact, the empirical results go in just the opposite direction. As the chart on page 93 shows, the Effort Index is a *better* predictor of peoples' positions on social welfare issues than is the Overall Index. Granted, the differences in the size of the coefficients, although consistent, are modest—necessarily so, since the Overall

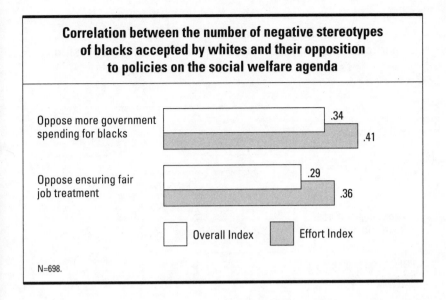

Correlation between the number of negative stereotypes of blacks accepted by whites and their opposition to policies on the social welfare agenda

Oppose more government spending for blacks
.34 Overall Index
.41 Effort Index

Oppose ensuring fair job treatment
.29 Overall Index
.36 Effort Index

☐ Overall Index   ▨ Effort Index

N=698.

Index overlaps the Effort Index. By way of revealing more clearly what is going on, we looked at the correlations between people's positions on social welfare issues of race and each of the negative racial stereotypes taken one at a time. The most striking aspect of the results, set out in the chart on page 94, is the remarkable variations in the magnitude of the coefficients of different stereotypes. For example, whether whites perceive blacks as having a chip on their shoulder has virtually nothing to do with whether they will support or oppose either an increase in government spending to help blacks or government oversight to ensure fair treatment in employment for blacks. Similarly, whether a white perceives blacks as more violent than whites is only trivially related to the likelihood that he or she will believe that government has no business trying to ensure that blacks get fair treatment in employment or that blacks ought to take care of their problems on their own. But when we consider the correlation between whites' perception that blacks who are on welfare could get a job if they really tried and the positions whites take on whether government spending in behalf of blacks should be increased or not, we find it to be emphatic. And the correlation between this perception of blacks and opposition to government oversight in employment, also shown in the chart, is virtually as strong. Moreover, the same

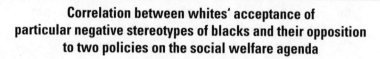

Correlation between whites' acceptance of particular negative stereotypes of blacks and their opposition to two policies on the social welfare agenda

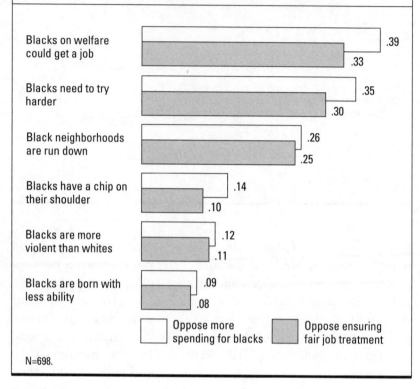

Blacks on welfare could get a job — .39 / .33

Blacks need to try harder — .35 / .30

Black neighborhoods are run down — .26 / .25

Blacks have a chip on their shoulder — .14 / .10

Blacks are more violent than whites — .12 / .11

Blacks are born with less ability — .09 / .08

☐ Oppose more spending for blacks ▨ Oppose ensuring fair job treatment

N=698.

holds for the second component of the Effort Index—the perception that if blacks would only try harder, they would be just as well off as whites. Whites who do not think blacks are trying as hard as they could or should are good bets to oppose more government spending for blacks and broader government oversight in employment in behalf of blacks. As the results make plain, *what matters are the particular stereotypes people accept about blacks.* The image of the violent black makes little difference to the positions whites take on whether government should provide social welfare assistance for blacks. But the image of the black who fails to make an effort counts for a lot.

These results point to an irony of the contemporary politics of race that has escaped attention altogether. In general, the milder the negative characterization of blacks, the more whites will agree with it; conversely, the nastier a racial stereotype, the fewer will endorse it. As we saw in Chapter 2, far more whites believe that blacks are not making as much of an effort to deal with their problems as they could or should than believe that blacks are belligerent or violent. But the point precisely to emphasize is that of the two stereotypes the milder—of not making a sufficient effort—is more immediately relevant to a judgment about government assistance, hence more potent politically, than the nastier one. Since the perception of blacks as failing to try hard, in part because it is less nasty than a characterization of blacks as violent, is more widespread, the paradoxical result is that less nasty stereotypes can do more damage politically than nastier ones.

Would the results be the same in another part of the country? Would they hold up if a more varied list of characteristics commonly attributed to blacks was measured? By way of addressing these concerns, a validational study deliberately varied both the stereotypes assessed and the geographical region. This study, taking advantage of a representative sample in Lexington, Kentucky, in 1989, expanded greatly the array of characterizations made of blacks. Of the ten different characterizations, five were positive ("family-oriented," "intelligent," "hard-working," "friendly," and "self-disciplined") and five were negative ("arrogant," "lazy," "irresponsible," "pleasure-loving," and "violent").

The crucial issue is whether opposition to a proposal on the social welfare issue is inspired by negative stereotypes of blacks indiscriminately or driven in particular by perceptions of blacks as failing to make a genuine effort to overcome their problems and to get ahead. The results, shown in the chart on page 96, are strikingly consistent with our other findings. Whites who describe blacks as hard-working are very supportive of increased government spending for them, whereas those who describe them as lazy oppose it strongly. On the other hand, there is essentially no connection between the positions whites take on government spending for blacks and whether they perceive blacks to be friendly, pleasure-loving, or family-oriented. In short, the results of the two studies are squarely consistent. Perceive blacks to be hard-working, and you will be inclined to support more government spending for them; perceive them to be lazy, and you will be inclined to oppose it, and whether you think well or ill of them in

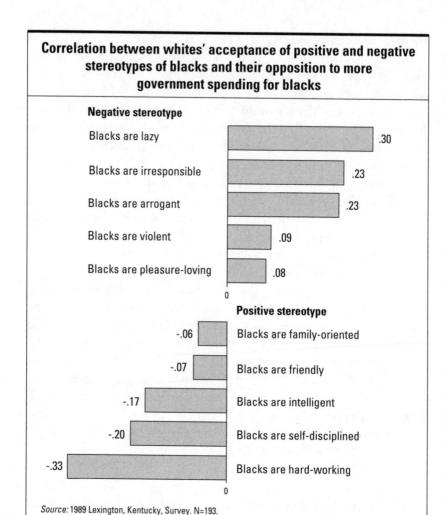

Correlation between whites' acceptance of positive and negative stereotypes of blacks and their opposition to more government spending for blacks

Negative stereotype

Blacks are lazy	.30
Blacks are irresponsible	.23
Blacks are arrogant	.23
Blacks are violent	.09
Blacks are pleasure-loving	.08

0

Positive stereotype

-.06	Blacks are family-oriented
-.07	Blacks are friendly
-.17	Blacks are intelligent
-.20	Blacks are self-disciplined
-.33	Blacks are hard-working

0

Source: 1989 Lexington, Kentucky, Survey. N=193.

other respects makes little difference for the position you take on social welfare policies.

But what does this pattern of selective association tell us about the politics of race? Not that whether whites perceive blacks to be violent or aggressive is unimportant. But what counts as a relevant reason for supporting or opposing a racial policy is defined in part by the policy itself. Quite apart from this, our findings show how self-deceptive it is to reduce arguments over racial policies just to prejudice. It is comforting, in a perverse way, to pin responsibility on racial prejudice, because it implies that the source of difficulty is only the bigot, and surely time and effort will overcome raw prejudice.

The problem, we want to suggest, is more serious. Opposition to social welfare assistance, our results make plain, goes beyond the ranks of bigots. Substantial numbers of whites who are not prejudiced—as measured by the total number of negative racial stereotypes they accept—nevertheless believe that blacks could be better off if they tried harder. They are people who acknowledge that blacks have been unfairly treated in the past, and indeed still suffer some disadvantages; they are not given to belittling or derogating outgroups; but they nonetheless believe that a measure of responsibility for the problems that blacks now experience must be shouldered by blacks themselves. And this judgment carries as much weight in shaping their view of welfare assistance for blacks as it does among whites who are manifestly prejudiced.

So how do whites make decisions about whether blacks are entitled to more social welfare assistance? By judging according to the "effort principle." The person faced with problems in part of his own making, who is not making a genuine effort to deal with them, is not entitled to assistance from others. The effort principle thus involves a pair of elements—judgments about the reasons for the problem besetting a person, and judgments about the effort a person is making to overcome the problem. Both judgments can be of consequence, but the second captures the aspect of reciprocity integral to ideas of fairness: one is not obliged to make a sacrifice to make things better for others if they are not also willing to make a sacrifice to make things better for themselves; conversely, one ought to make an effort in behalf of people who are trying to make an effort in behalf of themselves. And of course, the way to tell if a person is making a genuine effort is by how hard he or she is willing to work.

THE RACE-CONSCIOUS AGENDA

Prejudice drives the opposition of whites to efforts to improve the economic and social position of blacks, in the opinion of a number of commentators, nowhere more blatantly than in the case of affirmative action—indeed, so much so that opposition to affirmative action is said to be, in and of itself, racism. At one level, it is easy to understand how commentators can fall into this form of argument. Affirmative action is, manifestly, an issue about which many people have strong feelings, and it is tempting to infer that the reason the issue arouses such intense emotions is because it excites deep-seated, often denied, negative feelings about blacks. But to suppose that the positions that whites take on affirmative action are driven by prejudice mistakes entirely the fundamental basis of their reactions.

It would be foolish to suggest that how whites feel about blacks is entirely separated from their reactions to affirmative action, if only because the relatively small number of whites who support affirmative action out of principle will tend naturally to be sensitive to any characterization that slights blacks. But it is crucial, if one wants to understand the contemporary politics of race, to appreciate how comparatively slight is the impact of negative characterizations in shaping the positions that whites take on affirmative action. As the results in the chart on page 99 show (particularly the multiple correlation showing the cumulative effect), far from prejudice controlling the reactions of whites to affirmative action, the influence of negative characterizations of blacks is conspicuous by its modesty compared with its impact on whites' responses to more government spending for blacks.

Nor is affirmative action exceptional. The positions whites take on fair housing overlap comparatively little with their perceptions of blacks. And the same holds for the issue of busing, as the chart on page 100 makes plain. (The multiple correlations in both cases are only about .25.) We should emphasize that this pair of racial issues was picked precisely to provide a contrasting pair of racial policies, one markedly unpopular racial policy, busing, the other comparatively popular, fair housing. In neither case, however, are the results at all consistent with the conventional notion that whites' opposition to issues of race is being predominantly driven by raw prejudice.

But if it is not true that whites' opposition to the new race-conscious agenda is primarily rooted in prejudice, it is nonetheless true that there is a relation between how whites feel about blacks and how willing they are to support a policy like affirmative action. The size of the relation is not large, but its direction is

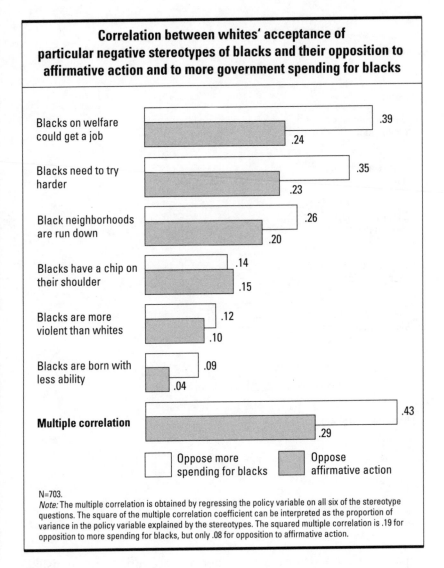

Correlation between whites' acceptance of particular negative stereotypes of blacks and their opposition to affirmative action and to more government spending for blacks

Blacks on welfare could get a job
.39
.24

Blacks need to try harder
.35
.23

Black neighborhoods are run down
.26
.20

Blacks have a chip on their shoulder
.14
.15

Blacks are more violent than whites
.12
.10

Blacks are born with less ability
.09
.04

Multiple correlation
.43
.29

☐ Oppose more spending for blacks   ▨ Oppose affirmative action

N=703.
Note: The multiple correlation is obtained by regressing the policy variable on all six of the stereotype questions. The square of the multiple correlation coefficient can be interpreted as the proportion of variance in the policy variable explained by the stereotypes. The squared multiple correlation is .19 for opposition to more spending for blacks, but only .08 for opposition to affirmative action.

always the same: whites who think less of blacks are less likely to support affirmative action.

But what is cause and what is effect? Surely the answer is obvious—people who dislike blacks therefore dislike going out of their way to help blacks; whites dislike affirmative action because they dislike blacks. But on reflection, another possibility becomes

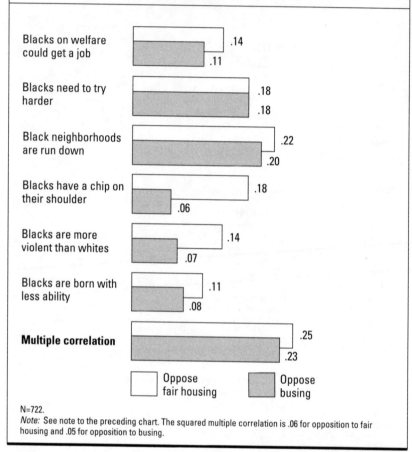

Correlation between whites' acceptance of particular negative stereotypes of blacks and their opposition to fair housing laws and to busing

Blacks on welfare could get a job
- Oppose fair housing: .14
- Oppose busing: .11

Blacks need to try harder
- Oppose fair housing: .18
- Oppose busing: .18

Black neighborhoods are run down
- Oppose fair housing: .22
- Oppose busing: .20

Blacks have a chip on their shoulder
- Oppose fair housing: .18
- Oppose busing: .06

Blacks are more violent than whites
- Oppose fair housing: .14
- Oppose busing: .07

Blacks are born with less ability
- Oppose fair housing: .11
- Oppose busing: .08

Multiple correlation
- Oppose fair housing: .25
- Oppose busing: .23

☐ Oppose fair housing   ▨ Oppose busing

N=722.
Note: See note to the preceding chart. The squared multiple correlation is .06 for opposition to fair housing and .05 for opposition to busing.

apparent. Can it also work the other way around? Can the dislike many whites feel for affirmative action lead them to dislike blacks?

Affirmative action excites strong feelings, passionate responses. An observer of the contemporary political climate cannot help but be struck by the intensity of many people's feelings about affirmative action. It is far from a rare experience to witness that people become agitated when discussing racial quotas or preferential treatment. And given the intensity of their emotions, it is not hard to see how they might wind up feeling less sympathetic, more negative, toward blacks. Without denying that a dislike of blacks can provoke dislike of policies to help blacks, it is also possible that dislike of a policy like affirmative action can provoke a dislike of blacks.

The possibility that affirmative action is itself creating some measure of ill will toward blacks deserves serious consideration. But how can one tell whether this is true? Certainly not by conventional studies of race and politics. In the standard public opinion survey, one can calculate accurately enough the correlation between dislike of affirmative action and dislike of blacks, but previous studies have not been designed to determine authoritatively which is cause and which is effect.

Accordingly, we have taken an altogether new route. Imagine two conversations about blacks and about affirmative action carried out at two different moments in time. We want to assume, for the sake of argument, that everything about these two conversations is the same—the two people who are talking to each other, the circumstances in which they are having their conversation, their mood of the moment. There is only one difference. The first time they talk about affirmative action, they then go on to talk about their sense of what blacks are like—whether they are hardworking, trustworthy, and the like. The second time, however, they talk about the same things but in exactly the opposite order, first expressing their views on blacks, then turning to the subject of affirmative action. And the crucial question we want to ask, taking advantage of this thought experiment, is this: Are they more likely to evaluate blacks negatively in the first conversation than the second? Intuitively imagining the two conversations, we want to suggest that they will respond more negatively to blacks in the first conversation than in the second, and the reason for their more negative response is the fact that they have just talked about affirmative action, and that has got them riled up. The thought of government jobs being given to blacks who have scored lower on civil service tests than whites who then have to go without work gets them angry; and that anger is partly vented when they go on to give their views of what blacks are like. But is it possible to scientifically evaluate this intuition?

We devised a special experiment—called the mere mention experiment—to simulate the kinds of conversations that ordinary people undoubtedly have about affirmative action and the characteristics of blacks. The basic idea is to take advantage of the power of randomization to determine whether references to affirmative action can, in and of themselves, excite negative reactions to blacks. The logic of the experiment runs like this. A random sample of a cross section of whites is randomly divided into two halves. One half is asked their view of affirmative action, then their images of blacks. The other half is asked exactly the same questions, except in the opposite order. If a dislike of affirmative action provokes a dislike of blacks, then the half of the sample of whites asked first about affirmative action should dislike blacks more than the other half. And, if the two halves are observed to differ in this way, the reason must necessarily be that the *mere mention* of affirmative action encourages dislike of blacks—necessarily so, since the two halves of the sample, being randomly composed, are alike in all respects, chance variations aside.

By affirmative action we mean not simply making an extra effort to see that qualified blacks are given consideration—which is in itself not an especially controversial policy—but rather ensuring that a predetermined proportion of jobs or college admissions go to blacks, whether or not they are the most qualified applicants. Accordingly, the question used in the experiment ran as follows:

> In a nearby state, an effort is being made to increase dramatically the number of blacks working in state government. This means that a large number of jobs will be reserved for blacks, even if their scores on merit exams are lower than those of whites who are turned down for the job. Do you favor or oppose this policy?

Notice that the question targets affirmative action not in the respondent's own state but rather in a "nearby state." The issue is framed in this way to eliminate, or at any rate to minimize, considerations of self-interest—to ensure, that is, that people do not object to affirmative action because they will themselves be cut out of a job. In the same survey, to measure whites' feelings toward blacks, we presented respondents with a number of descriptions of blacks, one half positive, the other half negative, prefacing our question with the qualification that of course no statement is true about everybody, but still, speaking generally, did they agree or disagree with these descriptions of blacks.

What we found was that merely asking whites to respond to the issue of affirmative action increases significantly the likelihood that they will perceive blacks as irresponsible and lazy. As the chart on page 104 shows, 43 percent of those who had just been asked their opinion about affirmative action described blacks as irresponsible, compared with only 26 percent of those for whom the subject of affirmative action had not yet been raised—a difference that is statistically significant. Analogously, whites who have been asked about affirmative action are more likely than those who have not heard the issue explicitly mentioned to describe blacks as lazy, by a difference of 31 to 20 percent. For that matter, whites who have just been asked to react to the race-conscious agenda are more likely to describe blacks as arrogant, though this difference is not statistically significant. Merely raising the issue of affirmative action, it is plain, increases the likelihood that whites will respond more negatively to blacks, not to an overwhelming extent and not in every respect, to be sure, but discernibly and precisely in the ways that most influence the reactions of whites to other racial policies, most especially those on the social welfare agenda.

In weighing the results of the mere mention experiment, it is essential to be clear on what is *not* being argued. It would be silly—and contrary to the results of the experiment—to assert that the primary reason that most whites dislike blacks is because they dislike affirmative action. Large numbers of whites endorsed negative characterizations of blacks before affirmative action came on the scene, and indisputably if affirmative action had never been dreamt of, substantial numbers would still accept negative racial stereotypes. Affirmative action did not create the problem of prejudice.

But it can aggravate it. Indeed, in reviewing the results of the mere mention experiment and in particular in gauging the size of the effects, the point to underline is that any effect at all was

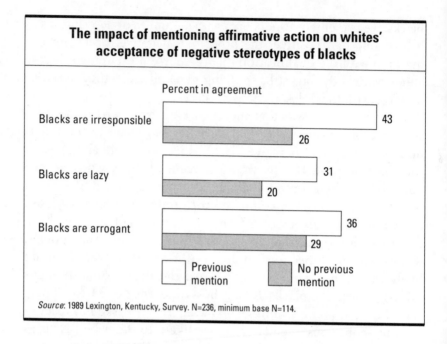

The impact of mentioning affirmative action on whites' acceptance of negative stereotypes of blacks

Percent in agreement

Blacks are irresponsible — 43 / 26

Blacks are lazy — 31 / 20

Blacks are arrogant — 36 / 29

☐ Previous mention ▨ No previous mention

Source: 1989 Lexington, Kentucky, Survey. N=236, minimum base N=114.

observed. The whole of the experimental "manipulation," after all, consisted in asking a question in an interview—only one question, in a standard form, in an interview made up of a hundred questions. No effort was made to whip up feelings about affirmative action. Respondents were not shown the equivalent of a "Willie Horton" type advertisement. They were not even subjected to a lengthy discussion of racial quotas or preferential treatment, to arouse latent feelings they might harbor. All that was done was to ask them a single question about affirmative action "in a nearby state." And that was sufficient to excite a statistically significant response, demonstrating that dislike of particular racial policies can provoke dislike of blacks, as well as the other way around.

RACIAL POLICIES AND RACIAL STEREOTYPES

We want to draw together some of the principal strands of the analysis, and in particular to consider the light this chapter's findings shed on the role of prejudice in shaping the contemporary politics of race.

At the outset, we want to make one point altogether clear. The question is not whether racial prejudice persists. It does, as indeed we have taken pains in Chapter 2 to demonstrate. The question here is a different one. It is: How far are the responses of whites to political issues of race dominated by racial prejudice?

For those who care about racism, and who wish to see it overcome, it has seemed important to insist that prejudice remains a powerful force in the thinking of white Americans. This insistence arises partly for intellectual reasons—why else would whites persist in opposing policies intended to redress generations of discrimination but for prejudice?—and partly for moral reasons—how else to convey the uniquely unfair burdens under which blacks labor? And as we have shown, prejudice *is* a significant factor. It is, if not the most important source of negative racial stereotypes, then one of the most important, as signaled by the striking overlap of negative stereotypes of blacks and Jews we observed in Chapter 2. And it is these negative stereotypes, or rather a crucial subset of them, which are closely tied up in whites' reactions to social welfare policies that benefit blacks, as we saw in this chapter.

All of this is true, and yet it misses the point why disagreements over racial issues need to be thought through afresh. For framing the problem as one of prejudice suggests that the source of difficulty lies with that segment of the American public who are bigots. There remain bigots, and they are not politically well-disposed toward blacks, but if the opposition to efforts to improve the social and economic position of blacks through government action consisted only, or even primarily, of bigots, the problem of race would be far less pervasive than it is. Indeed, what we want to suggest is that, paradoxically, thinking of the problem of race politics as a problem of prejudice trivializes the difficulties, because most of the people who oppose more government spending on behalf of blacks are not bigots.

What counts in generating opposition to policies to improve the social and economic position of blacks through government action is not any old negative characterization, but particularly the stereotype of the lazy, irresponsible black. It is nastier to talk about violent blacks than lazy blacks, but the latter stereotype is far more politically consequential than the former, as we have seen. Perceive blacks as belligerent or violent—it makes little or no difference in deciding whether to support or oppose more government spending to assist them. On the other hand, perceive blacks to be failing to make a genuine effort to overcome their problems, and one will be markedly more likely to oppose social welfare programs to help blacks. And the crucial point is that precisely those negative characterizations of blacks that count for most politically are the ones most commonly in circulation; and they are most common because of the contemporary circumstances that give them the color of plausibility.

It is part of the ordinary experience of many whites to encounter blacks who are not trying as hard as they could to overcome their problems—to know, at first hand or through the media, that black children disproportionately are dropping out of school, that black females are disproportionately having illegitimate children, that black families are disproportionately on welfare. All of these are social facts—facts that are rooted ultimately in the historical exploitation that blacks have suffered. But for many the crucial point is that these *are* social facts, and increasingly facts for which blacks are seen by ordinary white citizens to have to bear some responsibility, not for the problems' having arisen in the first place but for their persisting or even getting worse. And the consequence, as we saw in Chapter 2, is that exceedingly high proportions of whites—and for that matter, blacks, too—perceive blacks to be failing to make a genuine effort to work hard and overcome their problems on their own. Thus the impact of this common negative characterization of blacks on the political thinking of white Americans extends beyond—well beyond—the ranks of the manifestly bigoted.

Given the importance of this argument, we want to assess its validity from yet another angle. The logic of our test runs like this. Suppose we have at our disposal an infallible detector, on the basis of which we can assign people to one of two piles. One pile consists of all whites who are prejudiced, the other of all whites who are not. Broadly, what we should expect to find is, first, that whites who are prejudiced are more likely than whites who are not prejudiced to agree that blacks are not working as hard as they could to get ahead—perhaps twice as likely—and second, that whites who perceive blacks not to be trying as hard as they could will be more likely to oppose more government assistance for blacks *whether they are prejudiced against them or not.* Since there is no infallible device to detect prejudice, it is necessary to take advantage of an imperfect proxy. Given our belief that the heart of prejudice is captured by the notion of ethnocentrism, our measure of prejudice will be anti-Semitism, and whites will be sorted into not two but three piles, to isolate even better those who are most and least anti-Semitic.

Our argument is that perceptions of blacks as failing to make an effort count for as much in shaping reactions to social welfare issues for whites who are not prejudiced as for whites who are. And this is indeed what the results show. By way of illustration, consider the correlation between (1) believing that blacks could be as well off as whites if only they tried harder and (2) opposing more government spending programs to assist blacks (top right in the chart on page 108). The correlation between the two for the least prejudiced is virtually as large as for the most prejudiced (as measured by anti-Semitism). The same can be said for the positions whites take on whether government should ensure fair treatment in employment for blacks (top left). What is more, whenever the impact of stereotypes on racial policy preferences differs for the most and least prejudiced, the differences are in the opposite direction from what we would expect if prejudice were solely at the root of opposition to government assistance. Thus, the correlation between a perception of blacks as taking advantage of welfare and opposing more spending for blacks (bottom right) is almost twice as large for whites who are not prejudiced as for those who are.

All this further strengthens the argument that the central problem of racial politics is *not* the problem of prejudice. Bigotry provides a temptingly simple cause for a complex problem; it underlines the moral appeal of working to overcome the legacy of slavery and discrimination by fixing attention on the evil originally responsible for it. And not least, it fixes responsibility for the persistence of the problem on "them"—on the out-and-out bigots—in the process diverting attention from "us." There *are* bigots; and although their number is lower now than a generation ago, bigots are in no danger of becoming an extinct species. But to concen-

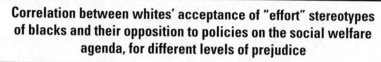

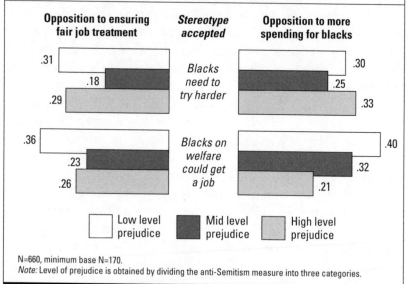

Correlation between whites' acceptance of "effort" stereotypes of blacks and their opposition to policies on the social welfare agenda, for different levels of prejudice

Opposition to ensuring fair job treatment	Stereotype accepted	Opposition to more spending for blacks
.31 / .18 / .29	*Blacks need to try harder*	.30 / .25 / .33
.36 / .23 / .26	*Blacks on welfare could get a job*	.40 / .32 / .21

Low level prejudice   Mid level prejudice   High level prejudice

N=660, minimum base N=170.
Note: Level of prejudice is obtained by dividing the anti-Semitism measure into three categories.

trate attention on the deviant and marginal in American life is to miss the larger problem. Many of the very reasons that blacks need government action—the problems of crime and unemployment and drugs and illegitimacy and educational failure—have also helped reinforce an image of blacks as failing to try as hard as they could or should. It is, of course, possible to turn around and insist that anyone who believes that blacks could be better off if they tried harder is a bigot. But it won't do to play Humpty Dumpty in *Alice in Wonderland*, insisting that words mean whatever one wishes them to mean. Blacks are as likely as whites to accept characterizations of blacks as failing to try hard, as we saw in Chapter 2, and unless one is prepared to say that blacks are just as prejudiced against blacks as are whites, it is necessary to accept the fact that a number of whites who are *not* prejudiced nonetheless have come to believe that part of the responsibility for the problems blacks face rests with blacks themselves.

This is, it should be said explicitly, only one illustration of a larger lesson to be drawn from our findings. Above everything else, if one wants to understand the issue of race in America in the 1990s as it actually is, it is necessary to acknowledge the complexity of the problem. Prejudice is at work, and there are still questions of race that have moral issues at their center. But the politics of race is complex, and the findings in this chapter have underlined its complexity. For one, it turns out that nasty racial stereotypes count for little politically, and less nasty ones can count for a lot. For another, although it has become fashionable to assert that opposition to affirmative action is driven by racism, as though the reason so many whites object to racial quotas and preferential treatment is prejudice pure and simple, it turns out that the politics of affirmative action has remarkably little to do with whites' feelings toward blacks. On the other hand, although little attention has been given to the politics of bread-and-butter social welfare issues, it turns out that this is precisely the policy agenda most heavily shaped by people's negative images of blacks.

The politics of race is driven not only by racial sentiments but also by politics—indeed, to a degree, racial politics is driving racial sentiments. If whites decide their position on issues of race partly on the basis of what they think about blacks, it is also true that what they think of policies devised to assist blacks influences what they think of blacks. Politics shapes as well as reflects public opinion, as the politics of affirmative action painfully demonstrates: whites have come to think less of blacks, to be more likely to perceive them as irresponsible and lazy merely in consequence of the issue of affirmative action being brought up. With the battle to persuade whites that blacks should be treated the same as whites only partly won, the political agenda raced on, fashioning a set of policies demanding, as a matter of principle, that blacks should be treated better than whites—that a black should be admitted to a school or get a job in preference to a white even if the white has higher grades or superior work skills. The new race-conscious agenda has provoked broad outrage and resentment. Affirmative action is so intensely disliked that it has led some whites to dislike blacks—an ironic example of a policy meant to put the divide of race behind us in fact further widening it.

5

THREE AGENDAS

White Americans are moved by a swirl of concerns and principles in responding to contemporary issues of race. We want now to trace out the patterns of their thinking, attending to the variety of elements they take into account—from abstract ideologies to raw prejudice—and analyzing the variety of the connections they draw among them. In particular, we want to make plain how the shape of their thinking about issues of race—the considerations they take into account and the weight they give them—reflects the shape of the particular racial issues they confront.

We shall begin with the politics of social welfare. The broad objective of the welfare agenda is to ameliorate the social and economic conditions of the disadvantaged. To that end an array of means are proposed, from programs like Head Start, through food stamps, through housing and education subsidies, through Aid to Families with Dependent Children. The common thread, though, is a desire to relieve the worst of the suffering the worst off suffer and to put in their hands the resources they need to make their own way. From the point of view of the larger public, then, the root issue defining the politics of social welfare is when people are obliged to take care of their own problems and when they are entitled to assistance at others' expense.

In responding to issues of social welfare, citizens at least partly base their judgments on their sense of what fairness requires of them. But precisely what makes the politics of race complex is that fairness means different things for different policy areas. The question is thus not just whether whites respect their standards of what is right in taking positions on issues of race; it is that the standards of what is right are not the same in all policy areas.

Social welfare policies constitute a major part of the politics of race, and we shall identify the specific standards ordinary citizens consider in deciding whether blacks should receive government assistance. But the question of whether the government should underwrite a program like Head Start or provide food supplements is a different kind of question from whether it should make it a criminal offense for a homeowner to refuse to sell his house to a black because he is black. The nub of fair housing is not whether blacks should be able to obtain a benefit, or claim a right, that others cannot; nor whether they should obtain a benefit under more generous terms than others can; only whether blacks should be able to do what most other Americans can do, and believe they have a clear right to do—to live where they want and can afford. The issue of fair housing laws centers on the principle not of government benefits but of equal treatment.

The issue of fair housing raises the principle of equal treatment in a particular context; indeed, it is an issue in large part because it pits the principle of equal treatment against the principle of property rights, where the right to property takes a form—owning their own house—that nearly all ordinary citizens either exercise or want to exercise. But that is only another way of saying that the choice citizens are asked to weigh when it comes to outlawing racial discrimination in the sale of housing is not the same as the choice they are asked to make about providing food stamps or other direct benefits.

Race-conscious policies pose yet a different choice. Again, a principle of fairness is at issue, but fairness understood in terms quite different from questions of either social welfare or equal treatment. Affirmative action allocates jobs and the means to obtain them on the basis of race, and it would be a mistake to fail to recognize this. But affirmative action is, above all, a moral issue, and the issue of right and wrong is fundamental to both proponents and opponents of it.

The moral issues raised by preferential treatment and racial quotas define the politics of affirmative action. Because issues of fundamental fairness are involved in a way they are not in other domains of race, the race-conscious agenda has a distinctive temper. Preferential treatment excites resentment and anger that other issues of race do not, and it clashes with some of the very values that move Americans to support both the social welfare and the equal treatment agenda. It needs, in consequence, to be understood in its own terms.

Americans, asked to support a range of policies to assist blacks, are being asked to make a range of choices. The differences among these choices—between a policy to provide social welfare, or to assure equal treatment, or to use race-conscious standards—matter. And they matter because the forces that move white Americans—the values, standards of fairness, biases, and concerns—differ from one aspect of race to another. In this chapter we will examine some of those differences in the motivations that underlie white Americans' differential support of the three policy agendas.

THE SOCIAL WELFARE AGENDA

In speaking of the social welfare agenda, we use the term welfare broadly. We mean to refer not to just a narrow slice of programs but to the larger policy agenda organized around the direct assistance government ought to supply to the disadvantaged, which has been prominent in American politics since the New Deal. The politics of welfare assistance did not originate in questions of race. On the contrary, the modern stamp of American politics, and still more specifically the identification of the Democratic party with bread-and butter liberalism, was set by the Great Depression and the New Deal.

Nevertheless, issues of welfare form a central part of the contemporary politics of race. Economically, blacks are markedly worse off than whites. As Hacker reports, in 1990 the median income for white families was $36,915, for black families $21,423; 44.8 percent of black children lived in poverty—using the official federal formula defining poverty—compared with 15.9 percent of white children; unemployment rates were almost three times as high among blacks as among whites (11.3 percent compared with 4.1 percent). And, partly because blacks are worse off economically, they are worse off in a variety of other ways. For example, in 1990 infant mortality rates were twice as high among blacks as among whites, while in 1988, whites were twice as likely to have graduated from a college or university. It cannot come as a surprise, given the enormity of the problems to be addressed, that a prominent and persistent subject for debate has been the lengths to which government should go to assist blacks with their economic and social problems.

When people go about making up their minds whether others are entitled to receive government assistance, the issue is only secondarily whether others *need* assistance; the primary issue for most people is whether those asking for assistance *deserve* it. And in making a determination whether others deserve assistance with their economic problems, a pair of rules help to define in the American culture who merits social welfare assistance: the "effort" principle, as we have seen, and the "fairness" principle.

By the "effort" principle, as we remarked in Chapter 4, we have in mind a moral rule of thumb which holds that people who make claims to assistance from others in dealing with their social or economic problems ought themselves to be making an effort to deal with their problems. It may not be within their power to overcome these problems entirely on their own. But to be in a position to ask others to make an effort in their behalf, they must at least be willing to try to make an effort on their own. In contrast, by the "fairness" principle, we have in mind the notion that people are entitled to government assistance in coping with social or economic problems if they are burdened with these problems not on their own account but because others have imposed them. Fairness consists in putting right unfairness.

In the minds of many people, this pair of principles—effort and fairness—provide a platform for judgments about who deserves welfare assistance. They are not conjured up out of thin air when the issue of welfare assistance for blacks comes under discussion; both principles tend to come into play in *any* discussion of welfare assistance. But that does not mean that the two principles are applied in the same way regardless of who is to receive assistance.

The principle of effort provides ample leeway for the impact of negative characterizations of blacks as irresponsible and as failing to try as hard as they could or should to deal with their problems. The ordinary citizen would be inclined to oppose welfare assistance to anyone he believes is not making a serious effort to help himself, but in the current climate of belief, this is how he is *likely* to perceive blacks. As we have seen in Chapter 2, striking numbers of whites, on the order of one in every two even in a liberal and affluent part of the country, perceive blacks as failing to try hard and as being irresponsible. And precisely those characterizations most immediately tied up with judgments about whether blacks deserve welfare assistance are the most prevalent.

To capture the fairness principle, we deployed a pair of questions. First:

> A history of slavery and being discriminated against has created conditions that make it difficult for black people to work their way up. Do you basically agree or basically disagree with that explanation as to why the average black American is not as well off as the average white American?

And second:

> Over the past few years, blacks have gotten less of the good things in life than they deserve. Do you basically agree or basically disagree with that statement?

Given the one-sided focus of recent research, which has concentrated on elements of the American culture that work against racial amity and omitted elements which work for it, it is important to point out that both these expressions of the fairness principle command marked public support. Specifically, in the Race and Politics Survey, approximately one in every two white Americans believes that blacks continue to get less of the good things in life than they deserve. Moreover, two in every three of them agree that it is harder for blacks to make their own way because of the discrimination and exploitation that they have suffered.

Furthermore, not only do large numbers of whites acknowledge that blacks have been, and continue to be, treated unfairly, but they also see a connection between the two—a connection which must be recognized if an acknowledgment of past injustices is not to degenerate into empty regret. Thus, whites who believe that slavery and discrimination in the past have made it hard for blacks to work their way up are likely also to take the position that the inequities of the past have continued even into the immediate present, with blacks continuing to get less of the good things than they should.

Even though Americans may agree on the two principles of effort and fairness that should underlie judgments about whether blacks are entitled to government assistance, their judgments about fairness or about effort are not made in a vacuum. White Americans disagree not about whether people who are making a genuine effort to deal with their problems on their own deserve assistance, but rather about whether *blacks* are making such an effort. Similarly, when it comes to the principle of fairness, the relevant disagreement is not over whether people who have been unfairly treated are entitled to help, but rather whether *blacks* continue to be treated unfairly.

How do whites make up their minds about the principles of effort and fairness applied to blacks? Why do some judge blacks to be making a genuine effort to cope with their problems on their own, while others perceive blacks to be coasting, unwilling to try as hard as they could or should? What leads some whites to affirm, and others to question, the claim that blacks are victimized by the legacy of discrimination and exploitation?

Surely the consideration to start with is prejudice itself. The positions Americans take on issues of race can be driven by prejudice in two different ways. They may oppose a particular racial policy—say, a proposal to increase government spending to assist blacks—out of prejudice *directly*. Their dislike of blacks leads them to reject policies to assist blacks, plain and simple. This conception of prejudice's impact on political thinking—direct, immediate—is very much the way the role of bigotry is ordinarily thought of. But in addition to its direct and immediate impact, prejudice also shapes political thinking in an *indirect*, roundabout way by shaping the factors that in turn shape the policy preferences of white Americans.

The other obvious factor to take into account is ideology, if only because the politics of welfare, certainly for those who know and care about politics, centers on ideology. Liberals and conservatives divide deeply over the nature, extent, and duration of the assistance government should provide individuals in coping with their problems—and therefore divide deeply over issues of assistance for blacks.

In saying that ideology may shape judgments about what government should do with respect to blacks, what comes to mind most immediately is the direct effect of ideology. So far as conservatism underlies skepticism of the ability of government to help individuals get on their own feet, it will encourage opposition to social welfare assistance for blacks. But in addition ideology also can exercise an indirect effect. For liberals and conservatives may also systematically differ in their application of the principles of fairness and effort, with the former more likely to perceive blacks as unfairly treated, the latter more likely to perceive blacks as failing to make a genuine effort to overcome their problems. In consequence, ideology should influence policy positions on racial welfare issues indirectly as well as directly.

We have, then, a variety of specific expectations about effort, fairness, prejudice, and ideology that need to be tied together rigorously, in order to yield a compelling account of how whites make up their minds whether to favor or oppose government assistance for blacks.

The causal models shown on page 117 posit that judgments about racial welfare issues are made in a two-step process. The first step of the process consists in making judgments of whether blacks are themselves making a genuine effort to deal with their problems, and whether blacks continue to be the victims of unfair treatment. If the answer is yes to either question, then whites will be inclined to favor social welfare assistance for blacks. But does the perception that blacks are being treated unfairly give rise to the belief that blacks are making a genuine effort, or does it work the other way around? Our contention is that judgments about whether blacks are making a genuine effort are made *prior*

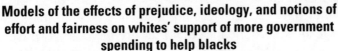

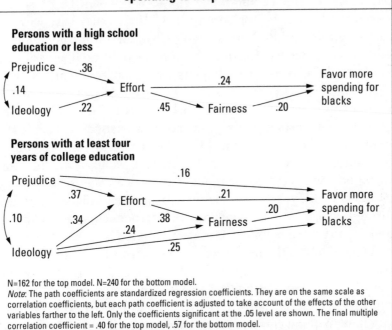

Models of the effects of prejudice, ideology, and notions of effort and fairness on whites' support of more government spending to help blacks

Persons with a high school education or less

Prejudice — .36
.14
Ideology — .22 → Effort — .24 → Favor more spending for blacks
.45 → Fairness — .20

Persons with at least four years of college education

Prejudice — .16
.37 → Effort — .21 → Favor more spending for blacks
.10 — .34 .38 .20
.24 → Fairness — .25
Ideology

N=162 for the top model. N=240 for the bottom model.
Note: The path coefficients are standardized regression coefficients. They are on the same scale as correlation coefficients, but each path coefficient is adjusted to take account of the effects of the other variables farther to the left. Only the coefficients significant at the .05 level are shown. The final multiple correlation coefficient = .40 for the top model, .57 for the bottom model.

to judgments about whether they are now fairly treated. It is not possible, with the data at hand, unequivocally to demonstrate this, and we recognize that others might reasonably take the opposite view. But it is more consistent with both previous research and common sense to assign priority to the effort principle in deciding whether blacks should receive government assistance. A white will tend to acquire a negative characterization of blacks as irresponsible and unwilling to work hard before acquiring particular beliefs about whether blacks have, or have not, been unfairly treated. Hence, judgments about the principle of effort are represented, in the models, as causally prior to judgments about the principle of fairness, and so perceptions of blacks as failing to make a determined effort to get ahead influence positions on welfare assistance in two ways—on their own, *directly*, and, by undercutting a belief that blacks are unfairly treated, *indirectly*.

Judgments about the characteristics of blacks, or of the treatment they have received, are not made in a vacuum. In particular, we want to explore the idea that they are driven by two factors in particular—prejudice and ideology—leaving open the possibility that the role of either or both of these factors may vary with the extent to which white Americans have had the advantage of formal education. When we describe a person as a political liberal or conservative, here as in other chapters we are taking them exactly at their word: the alternative is to impose an arbitrary definition of liberal and conservative, which risks "cooking" the results. And to tell whether they make a negative evaluation of blacks (for example, that they are not making a genuine effort) for reasons of prejudice, since consistency of dislike of outgroups is the signature of bigotry, we shall use our measure of anti-Semitism. Finally, consistent with previous research, we will take formal education as a rough gauge of the extent to which respondents form complex and sophisticated belief systems about politics.

The models in the figure convey our sense of how all these factors—prejudice, ideology, and judgments about effort and fairness—fit together. Prejudice, when it gains a hold on a person, is a fundamental factor in his or her thinking. To reflect this, we shall stipulate that any connection between it and any of the other factors must be taken as evidence of its importance in shaping the thinking of whites. The analysis thus credits prejudice with both direct and indirect effects on whites' political thinking. We also assume that people's overall political orientation is a more fundamental factor in their political thinking than specific judgments they may make about whether blacks are making a genuine effort or are being treated unfairly.

Our results show that whites tend to base their positions on social welfare assistance for blacks to a significant degree on judgments about effort and fairness. They are more likely to oppose increased government spending if they believe blacks are not making a genuine effort to deal with their own problems, and are more likely to support it if they believe blacks are unfairly treated. And this is true whether they have had relatively little education or a lot. Indeed, the person with a college degree is as likely to place importance on judgments of fairness and effort as the one who has had a high school education or less.

But how people go about reaching a position on social welfare issues manifestly varies with education. The most glaring difference is the role of ideology. Policy positions on social welfare issues are ideologically driven among the well educated, and, what is more, ideologically driven in three distinct ways. First, ideology influences the judgments well-educated people make about the effort principle, with liberals being more, and conservatives less, likely to perceive blacks to be making a genuine effort to deal with their problems and to get ahead. And judgments about effort in turn significantly influence the positions that people take on government assistance for blacks. Second, ideology influences the judgments people make about the fairness principle, with conservatives being more, and liberals less, likely to judge that blacks are being fairly treated; and judgments about fairness in turn influence the positions that people take on government assistance for blacks. Finally, as the bottom arrow running directly from ideology to more government spending makes plain, ideological identification also directly influences positions on social welfare issues, with liberals of course being more, and conservatives less, likely to support increased government spending to assist blacks.

In contrast, ideology has only a modest impact on the thinking of less-educated whites. There is a statistically significant connection between ideology and the judgments about the effort principle, but the connection is distinctly weaker for the less educated than for the more. Moreover, there is no direct impact of ideology on their policy preferences. Finally, there is no connection between ideological identification and their judgment on the fairness principle.

It is worth a moment, before continuing on with the record of specific results, to consider the larger point. Do differences like this matter? What do they tell us about the actual politics of race?

The very same issue, these results suggest, can have a very different politics in different parts of contemporary American society. The issue of government spending for blacks is thus a deeply ideological issue among the more aware and better educated, with liberalism and conservatism being primary forces exerting influence both on their own and by shaping Americans' application of both the fairness and effort principles to blacks. On the other hand, the political temper of the very same issue is quite different among the less aware and less educated. Ideology is *not* a major force shaping their reactions to the issue of government spending for blacks. The politics of the very same issue thus takes on a very different tone in different segments of society.

The politics of welfare is not just the politics of ideology. Prejudice also plays a part, and in all parts of American society, as the results in the figure make plain. Examining the model closely, one can see the principal way that prejudice shapes issue positions on government spending for blacks. It is by its impact on the application of the effort principle. The more prejudiced a person is, the more likely he or she is to perceive blacks to be failing to make a genuine effort to deal with their problems on their own; and insofar as a person perceives blacks to be failing in this way, he or she is in consequence more likely to oppose proposals to increase the level of government spending to help blacks. What is more, the indirect influence of prejudice on positions about government spending for blacks, through its shaping of the "effort" principle, is every bit as strong among the college educated as among the high school educated.

It is common to think of the impact of prejudice as diffuse, as coloring in a broad way whites' reasoning about issues of race. However, as the overall pattern of results of the causal analysis demonstrates, the impact of prejudice on political thinking is strikingly specific: of the two considerations of equity that people take into account in making up their minds about social welfare policies, prejudice colors whites' thinking about whether blacks are making a genuine effort but not their judgments about whether blacks are fairly treated. These results thus make explicit why characterizations of blacks as irresponsible and lazy are so consequential: because *they supply the principal channel through which the influence of prejudice on whites' opinions about social welfare policies flows.*

Viewed from another angle, the results also make plain where the revisionist view of race and ideology goes wrong. The new racism researchers' thrust has been to assert that ideology reduces to racism. A particular person may say that he objects to more government spending to help blacks because of the necessity for fiscal restraint, or perhaps because of the importance he attaches to the value of self-reliance: he may even believe sincerely what he says publicly. But according to the revisionist view, the bottom line is that conservative ideology is the handmaiden of racism: there has been a "conjunction" or "fusion" of the two. What we found is that *both* prejudice and ideology play a role in the politics of the social welfare agenda.

The necessary starting point, if one is to appreciate both the independence and the complementarity of prejudice and ideology, is to observe that the magnitude of the correlation between ideology and prejudice is essentially trivial. As the coefficients beside the curved arrows in the models indicate, there is scarcely any overlap between bigotry (assessed by anti-Semitism) and conservatism (assessed by ideological self-identification), whatever people's level of education. Granted, both prejudice and conservatism encourage the idea that blacks should take care of their problems on their own, as opposed to being entitled to receive assistance from others, and both do so by favoring a perception of blacks as failing to make a genuine effort to take care of their problems. But without discounting the role of prejudice, to suggest that conservatism reduces to racism gets the politics of welfare wrong. What stands out in the models is the multiplicity of ways that ideology exercises an impact on social welfare policy preferences among the college educated. Ideology influences perceptions of effort, and thereby issue preferences; it influences perceptions of fairness, and thereby issue preferences; and it influences issue preferences directly, without mediation at all. The politics of the social welfare agenda is the politics of ideology, not because ideology is the only relevant consideration, but rather because it tends to have an influence on most of the relevant considerations as well as exerting an influence in its own right.

THE EQUAL TREATMENT AGENDA

Our concern here is with a crucial issue of race: the issue of fair housing. The aim of fair housing legislation is to make illegal a refusal to sell or rent housing because of race, religion, and so on. To measure attitudes toward fair housing, we used the standard question developed by the General Social Survey:

Suppose there were a community-wide election on a general housing law and that you had to choose between two possible laws. One law says that homeowners can decide for themselves who to sell their houses to, even if they prefer not to sell to blacks. The second law says that homeowners are not allowed to refuse to sell to someone because of race or color. Which law would you vote for? That homeowners can decide for themselves who to sell to, or that homeowners can *NOT* refuse to sell to someone because of race or color?

Our objective is to capture the distinctive forces lying behind white Americans' reactions to antidiscrimination laws and to compare them with the factors driving white Americans' reactions to the social welfare agenda. Conservatism, we have seen, is a powerful factor shaping the opposition of all but the least educated to more government spending for blacks. By contrast, as the chart on page 123 makes plain, whatever whites' levels of education, the connection between their ideological orientation and their position on fair housing is conspicuous by its weakness, even among the most educated. The politics of welfare centers on ideology; the politics of fair housing does not.

A major reason why the distinctive character of different issues of race has not been recognized is that the vocabulary we customarily deploy exaggerates their similarity. Consider the idea of fairness. In focusing on the politics of welfare issues, we argued that fairness was a fundamental consideration, with whites more likely to favor government assistance for blacks if they believed that blacks had been unfairly treated. And support for antidiscrimination laws surely revolves around a notion of fairness, too: but— and this is the point that has been neglected—the notion of fairness which applies to the question of direct government assistance is not relevant to the issue of fair housing. Similarly, support for antidiscrimination laws, in some sense, is tied to a notion of desert on the part of blacks: but the notion of desert which applies to issues of welfare assistance is not relevant to the issue of fair housing. Ideas of what is fair and whether a person deserves assistance take particular shapes in the context of particular policies. Context matters and, consistent with this, the positions white Americans adopt on the issue of government spending are closely bound up with the positions they take on the principles of effort and fairness, as the chart on page 124 makes clear. In contrast, the positions they adopt on the issue of open housing are only modestly correlated with either the effort or the fairness principle. In short, the reasons why whites favor or oppose fair housing laws are

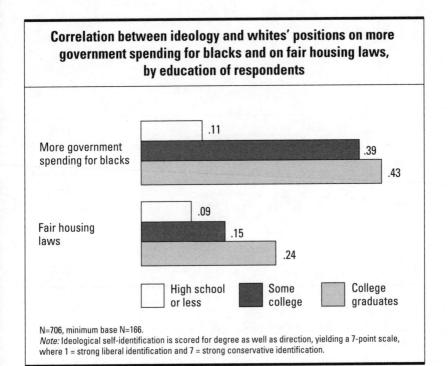

Correlation between ideology and whites' positions on more government spending for blacks and on fair housing laws, by education of respondents

More government spending for blacks
- .11
- .39
- .43

Fair housing laws
- .09
- .15
- .24

☐ High school or less   ■ Some college   ▨ College graduates

N=706, minimum base N=166.
Note: Ideological self-identification is scored for degree as well as direction, yielding a 7-point scale, where 1 = strong liberal identification and 7 = strong conservative identification.

only marginally related to the principal reasons they favor or oppose social welfare policies for blacks.

At the beginning of this study, we supposed, like nearly everyone else, that different issues of race did tend "to boil down to the same single question" of how whites felt about blacks, and therefore that whites would oppose fair housing laws for much the same reason they would oppose social welfare programs for blacks—because they disliked blacks. Only as examination of the data proceeded were we struck by the distinctiveness of a number of racial issues, including fair housing, although by then it was too late to incorporate measures of factors more specially relevant to questions of housing. For this reason, our account of the decision-making process in the case of fair housing is limited. In addition, although the politics of race in the San Francisco Bay Area is in many respects a microcosm of the politics of race in the country as a whole, the parallels are not perfect. And the divergence is especially marked in the climate of opinion surrounding the issue of fair housing. There is more support for fair housing in the Bay

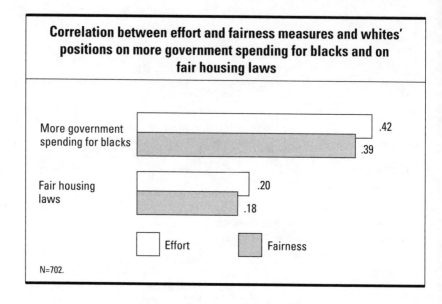

Correlation between effort and fairness measures and whites' positions on more government spending for blacks and on fair housing laws

More government spending for blacks
- Effort: .42
- Fairness: .39

Fair housing laws
- Effort: .20
- Fairness: .18

□ Effort ▨ Fairness

N=702.

Area—approximately three in every four whites support laws banning discrimination—than in the country as a whole. This is not surprising considering that the Bay Area is an uncommonly well-educated, affluent, and liberal part of the country, but it does underline the need to explore on a national basis the results we report here.

However that may be, the issue of fair housing poses a question of public policy different in kind from that posed by issues of welfare. The issue is not whether blacks should be given additional benefits in the form of direct payments, training programs, food stamps, or medical care. Rather, the issue is whether the force of the law should be employed to ensure that blacks are treated the same as whites, and specifically to ensure that they are not denied, merely because of the color of their skin, the same opportunity to buy a house or rent an apartment as anyone else.

The issue of fair housing thus centers on the principle of equal treatment—posed, however, in a quite specific context. The issue is not whether blacks should be treated the same as whites in the use of public parks or other public accommodations, nor whether they should be treated the same as whites in the exercise of civic rights such as the right to vote. What distinguishes fair housing on the equal treatment agenda is the call to use the force of law to back the principle of equal treatment in a "private" context—to intervene in decisions which people would ordinarily take to be their own business. It is the application of the principle of equal treatment, backed by the power of law, to choices once regarded as private that puts a distinctive stamp on the politics of fair housing.

A first step in characterizing this distinctive stamp is to underline the role of prejudice in shaping whites' positions on issues of fair housing laws. Bigotry is brought into play, if not by the appeal to use the force of law in behalf of blacks, then by the prospect of immediate, prolonged, and unavoidable everyday contact with blacks. The argument over open housing surely serves as a fundamental faultline dividing the racially tolerant from the racially intolerant. But it does not follow that differences of opinion over fair housing laws are entirely driven by prejudice. Perhaps less obviously, but also more consequentially, it does not follow that the argument over fair housing takes the same shape in all parts of contemporary American society. Even when a social norm forms in favor of equal treatment, it is not likely to be equally strong in all parts of society; and our intuition is that opposition to fair housing driven by prejudice will be strongest in the parts of American society where the norm of equal treatment is weakest.

How, exactly, might one assess the correctness of this intuition? One test is to calculate the impact of prejudice on reactions to fair housing for people with different levels of education. If a normative consensus has been reached on the principle of fair housing, then it should be the most educated who are the most likely to conform to it, the least educated who are the most likely to deviate from it—if only because they are the least likely to know of it. When we calculated the association between whites' prejudice (indexed by anti-Semitism) and their positions on the issue of fair housing for three different levels of education—those with a high school degree or less, those with some college, and those with either a bachelor's or advanced college degree, we found that the correlation between anti-Semitism and opposition to fair housing for the more educated is small, as shown in the chart on page 126; in contrast, the comparable correlation for the least educated is strikingly larger.

Two lessons should be drawn from this result. The first is that one of the potent factors lying behind opposition to fair housing,

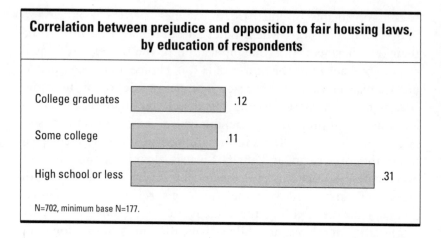

Correlation between prejudice and opposition to fair housing laws, by education of respondents

College graduates .12

Some college .11

High school or less .31

N=702, minimum base N=177.

even now, remains prejudice. The issues involved, particularly in forming a judgment of the importance of prejudice as a factor in reaching political decisions, are subtle. The estimates we have just seen should be read as conservative, if anything understating rather than overstating the role of prejudice. The impact of prejudice would be shown to be still larger, in all probability, if the measure had focused on relevant negative stereotypes about blacks rather than negative stereotypes about Jews. This is conjecture, to be sure, but plausible nonetheless. What is not conjecture, and the point we wished to drive home by choosing anti-Semitism as a measure of prejudice, is the blindness of the prejudice at work. Our finding that opposition to fair housing laws that protect blacks is tied up with people's negative feelings about Jews shows that this opposition has nothing to do with blacks as they are, and everything to do with bigotry.

A second lesson to derive from these results is that the issue of fair housing does centrally turn around prejudice—but not equally so in all strata of society. Prejudice has only a relatively modest direct effect among the more educated. The terms of argument over fair housing, as indeed over a number of racial issues, can differ in significant ways from one part of American society to another. The same issue which may hinge heavily on prejudice in one part of society may be only peripherally related to it in another. It is thus a fundamental error simply to ask: Is prejudice an important factor in contemporary politics or not? The question to ask is instead: For which racial issues, and for which parts of American society, is prejudice most important? For which least important?

If prejudice is not the reason that well educated and aware citizens oppose fair housing, then what is? What is the argument over fair housing about if it is not about intolerance? Among certain strata in American society, the division over fair housing reflects an argument over whether the power of law should be employed to assure equal treatment or equal opportunity. Even though the objective is equality of opportunity, not equality of result, the issue of government intervention is still open for debate. Some elements of the American ethos favor this form of government intervention, but there are others—also legitimate—which oppose it.

To assess the importance of people's ideas about the proper role of government in assuring equal treatment and equal opportunity, we used a question developed by the National Election Study. Specifically, a random half of the respondents in the Race and Politics Survey were asked whether they basically agree or disagree that:

While equal opportunity for women to succeed is important, it's not really the government's job to guarantee it.

It is our suspicion that some whites balk at making racial discrimination in housing illegal because they are reluctant to enlarge the areas in which government can intervene to define what is and is not allowed. But in suggesting this, we are far from asserting that the politics of open housing is shaped by concerns about the proper role of government throughout the public as a whole. The proper limits of government, although hardly an impossibly abstract issue, is not an everyday concern, and it seems only reasonable that concerns over the enlargement of governmental scope are most likely to be definite and to have had their implications thought through among those who are most engaged by politics and most adept at handling abstract ideas.

In fact, as the chart on page 128 shows, among the least educated, we found the connection between people's attitudes toward government guarantees of equal opportunity for women and their views on fair housing laws to be negligible. But with increases in educational level, the connection between the two grows tighter,

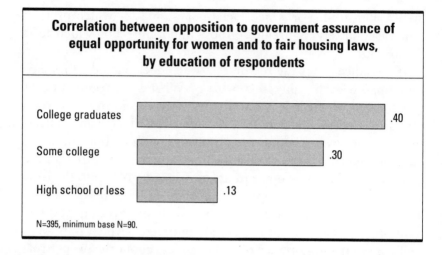

Correlation between opposition to government assurance of equal opportunity for women and to fair housing laws, by education of respondents

College graduates	.40
Some college	.30
High school or less	.13

N=395, minimum base N=90.

becoming substantial for those with some exposure to college, and strikingly large for those who have graduated from college.

The findings we have presented, strong as they are, do not amount to a full account of the politics of fair housing. Important aspects of people's reactions to the use of the law to enforce equal treatment remain to be explored. But even though part of the picture is incomplete, the outlines have been well defined, and they make plain that the politics of the equal treatment agenda are not interchangeable with those of the social welfare agenda. The principles of effort and fairness that define the willingness of white Americans to support social welfare assistance for blacks are not central to judgments about fair housing and equal treatment, and the elements that promote support for fair housing are not central to arguments over social welfare. The difference from one policy agenda to another in animating ideas is part of what we mean by the idea of issue pluralism. But these results have revealed another aspect of the idea. Simply put, the politics of the very same issue can also differ markedly from one part of American society to another.

THE RACE-CONSCIOUS AGENDA

Perhaps nowhere is it more important to recognize the pluralism of racial politics than in confronting the politics of affirmative action—nor less commonly done. Affirmative action, rather than being recognized as exceptional and to be understood in its own terms, has been taken to be the paradigm of racial politics, and opposition to it has been treated as synonymous with racism. This mischaracterizes both the politics of affirmative action and the politics of other racial agendas. We want now to focus on how the politics of the new race-conscious agenda differs from the politics of the older agendas of social welfare and equal treatment.

It is by no means unreasonable to view the "new" racial agenda as a continuation of the old. The new agenda excites controversy and is portrayed as radical and un-American, but so, too, was the old. The effort to permit a black to sip water from the same tap as a white was denounced as unconstitutional—indeed, as un-American—just as affirmative action is now denounced. Can it not be argued that affirmative action at its core is a continuation of the same desire to improve the circumstances of blacks? Isn't the opposition to it, at *its* core, just a new variation on a very old theme?

Myrdal suggested that the highest card to be played in the politics of civil rights, the one that would trump all the others, was the American Creed. The Creed summarized the ideals of Americans, and these ideals favored liberty and equality for blacks. It was just this—the identification of the political drive against legally mandated inequality and the normative thrust of the American Creed—that elevated the issue of race onto a different plane and made it so quintessentially a moral issue. Civil rights was not pork barrel politics: it was not just an effort to make blacks better off, but a larger crusade in behalf of what Americans, white as well as black, agreed is just.

One half century later the politics of race has lost a measure of its moral standing. This was to some extent inevitable with time and success, but the root causes go deeper. Beginning with the black separatism and nationalism of the 1960s, through the race-conscious programs of the 1980s, the relation between race as a public issue and the American Creed has been twisted on its axis. Far from the Creed being allied with all the causes championed in behalf of blacks, it is now at odds with some of them. Far from the race-conscious efforts being stamped by the Creed as fair and morally defensible, they are seen by many who uphold the

Creed—indeed by most—as unfair and morally wrong on their face.

This reversal of the relation between the American Creed and the new racial agenda is the key to the politics of affirmative action. We want therefore to explore the signal feature of the new racial agenda—its irony. The point at which to begin is to acknowledge that the new racial agenda is politically controversial precisely because most Americans do *not* disagree about it. The distribution of public opinion on issues of busing and affirmative action (understood as involving either preferential treatment or racial quotas), both in the NES national sample and in the RAP regional sample, is unmistakable. As the chart on page 131 shows, there is scarcely any support for either policy among whites. In the country as a whole, affirmative action in employment or in education is opposed by four in every five, or more. And the reactions of whites in the Bay Area, notwithstanding its reputation for being in the vanguard, are similarly one-sided. Only 27 percent of whites support racial quotas for college admissions; 73 percent oppose them. The story is much the same for the issue of busing: huge majorities in opposition, minorities in support. Even among blacks, opinion on busing was split fifty-fifty in the RAP survey. Still more dramatically, it was also split right down the middle on affirmative action. Aspects of the new racial agenda are difficult to swallow for many blacks as well as most whites.

In working through the politics of the new agenda, however, it is essential to avoid bewitchment by words. The term "affirmative action" is a potent stimulus. It is all the same an empty phrase to many in the public, whose meaning depends on context. Thus, a 1988 Harris Poll, which asked a random sample of the country as a whole whether they "favor or oppose affirmative action programs for blacks and other minorities, which do not have rigid quotas," found that 55 percent of whites favored affirmative action so defined—a level of public support in the same neighborhood as for the social welfare agenda. The idea of quotas and preferential treatment is the reef on which affirmative action founders.

It might be argued that the sticking point is the novelty, the unconventionality, of what is being proposed. To adjust scores on a civil service test, improving the results of a black and lowering those of a white merely on the grounds that one person is black

Whites' opposition to affirmative action and busing, nationally and in Bay Area

Percent opposed

Preference in hiring and promotion in jobs	90
Racial quotas for college admissions	76
	73
School busing	76

☐ Nationally   ▨ Bay Area

Source: 1986 National Election Study, N=767; 1986 Race and Politics Survey, N=773.

and the other is white, is a novel idea. And people may reject it for just this reason: because it is so different, so unexpected. To determine whether policy novelty is indeed the sticking point, we wanted to consider reactions to a racial policy just as novel as affirmative action—namely, set-asides. Set-asides are policies guaranteeing, as a matter of law, that a certain share of government business goes to minorities. By way of finding out public opinion on these policies, we asked whether:

> there should be a law to ensure that a certain number of federal contracts go to minority contractors.

But given our interest in the dynamics of racial policy preferences, instead of supposing that people had simply a fixed position, one way or the other, on set-asides, we wanted to see whether there was a greater willingness to go along with a racial policy if they knew it was not merely a possible course of action but the actual law of the land. After all, we reasoned, some additional people may be willing to support a racial policy knowing it is the law of the land, either because they think their views ought to conform to the law or because they suppose that, having been made into a law, a policy must have merit.

But how can this intuition be assessed? How can one determine if whites are more willing to go along with a policy if they know it is not merely a possible course of action but is the actual law of the land? The problem is trickier than it may seem. On the one hand, it is necessary to inform respondents that a policy has the backing of political leaders; on the other hand, in doing so it is essential to avoid provoking a merely partisan response. Suppose we were to say that the president favors set-asides, then we might well find Republicans to be less supportive, perceiving the policy to be the handiwork of a Democrat. To reduce the chances of a merely partisan reaction, and to evoke some of the prestige attached to national institutions, one half of the time the question on set-asides began:

The Congress of the United States—both the House of Representatives and the Senate—have passed laws

In contrast, the other half of the time the question began:

Sometimes you hear it said that there should be a law

The body of the question was exactly the same, and needless to say, the two introductions—the "law" and the "neutral" versions—were administered on a random basis.

The results of the appeal to law convey something of the elasticity of white attitudes toward issues of race, which we will examine in more detail in Chapter 6. As the chart on page 133 shows, when an appeal is made to the law as a persuasive symbol, approximately six in every ten say that set-asides are a good idea; in contrast, in the neutral version, only about four in every ten say they are a good idea. The difference is not only statistically but politically significant: appealing to the law as a persuasive symbol to build up support for the policy of set-asides transforms the policy from one backed by a minority—a large minority, but a minority all the same—into a policy backed by a clear majority.

These results illustrate an important lesson about the politics of race. Whites cannot be pushed and pulled at will in every direction. Nevertheless, on a number of racial issues, a sufficient number can be induced to support a policy to assist blacks to change the political status of the policy, from a course of action opposed by a majority of whites to one supported by a majority of whites. And in politics, this can be everything.

Impact of knowing that minority set-asides have been passed into law by Congress

Percent favoring set-asides

Told that it is the law	57
Not told that it is the law	43

N=773, minimum base N=369.

Having said this, it is also worth remarking the absolute levels of support for set-asides, even when no special inducement is given to support them. The issue is whether a certain number of federal contracts should be guaranteed to minority contractors. The practice of preferential treatment, even racial quotas, is logically implied, but obliquely; the suggestion is, rather, that the government should see that minorities are not left out altogether, and take the steps necessary to guarantee this. Roughly four in every ten whites support set-asides. This is less than a majority, to be sure, but it is a very substantial figure all the same. Given the tendency to focus on elements of public opinion that are unsympathetic to blacks, it is worth underlining the sizeable number of whites who believe the government should take an extra step, if necessary, to see that things go better for blacks.

The sticking point with affirmative action obviously cannot be novelty, since set-asides are as novel a policy approach as affirmative action, and yet they enjoy markedly more support than affirmative action. Why, then, is the reaction to affirmative action so distinctive? Is it because white Americans object to imposing quotas ιo benefit blacks? Or because citizens in general, whether Americans or not, object to the use of quotas, whether for blacks or not? As the chart on page 134 makes plain, we can see that the opposition to affirmative action is far from unique to the United States. Surveys reporting attitudes toward an array of policies to increase opportunity in education and employment, mounted in behalf of *women*, in Australia, Germany, Italy, the United Kingdom, and the United States, show similar results. In every country, giving women preferential treatment for jobs and promo-

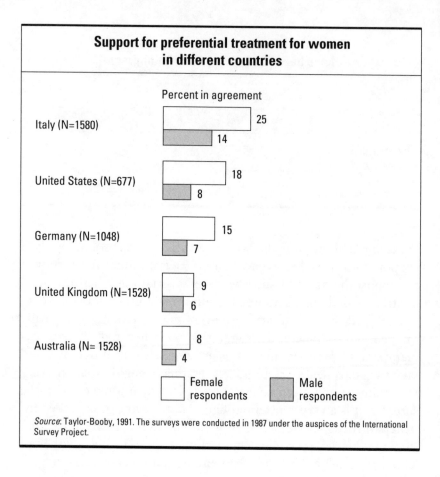

Support for preferential treatment for women in different countries

Percent in agreement

Italy (N=1580)
25
14

United States (N=677)
18
8

Germany (N=1048)
15
7

United Kingdom (N=1528)
9
6

Australia (N= 1528)
8
4

Female respondents

Male respondents

Source: Taylor-Booby, 1991. The surveys were conducted in 1987 under the auspices of the International Survey Project.

tions is massively unpopular. Consider the minuscule levels of support, first among men: in Australia, 4 percent; in the United Kingdom, 6; in Germany, 7; in the United States, 8; in Italy, 14. The comparable figures for women are: 8, 9, 15, 18, and 25. In short, affirmative action is opposed nearly as often by women, who would stand to benefit by it in this case, as by men, and it is overwhelmingly rejected by both.

As these results make plain, the reactions of white Americans to affirmative action are in no way unique. Proposing to privilege some people rather than others, on the basis of a characteristic they were born with, violates a nearly universal norm of fairness. It is in just this sense that differences over affirmative action go beyond race.

The politics of race have become complex, as the findings of this chapter have demonstrated. The politics of the social welfare and equal treatment agendas are not interchangeable, and the politics of both are distinct from those of the new race-conscious agenda. There are common elements, but the values and fears and convictions about fairness and equality that fire people's minds about affirmative action differ profoundly from those that move them to take one or the other side on matters of social welfare or equal treatment.

These differences matter, not least because they affect the way the record of the last three decades ought to be read. The common presumption is that the civil rights movement has proceeded in two stages, concerned first to secure equal treatment for blacks, then, with the passage of the civil rights laws of the 1960s, dedicated to the race-conscious agenda. The suggestion is that the more straightforward aspects of racial equality were first taken care of, then the movement moved on to more controversial and morally ambitious programs such as affirmative action.

This misreads the politics of race. The silent, tacit implication that the battles of the first phase have been resolved, and that the active battle has now moved on to the second phase, to the fight in behalf of affirmative action and not simply equal treatment, is wrong—quite wrong. A large part of what it means to say that the politics of race is complex now in a way it was not a generation ago is precisely that the old battles *as well as* the new ones are being fought. Our findings on fair housing demonstrate that white Americans still *remain* divided over what should be done to assure equal treatment, a fundamental fact about the contemporary politics of race that has been lost from sight because of the attention paid to the most readily visible, and obviously controversial, of the three agendas—the race-conscious agenda. And just this is responsible for much of the irony, and part of the tragedy, of the contemporary politics of race.

6

CHANGING MINDS
ABOUT RACE

The commitment of many Americans to racial equality is qualified and conflicted—it could hardly be otherwise given the swirl of values and concerns stirred up by race-related issues, from affirmative action to welfare dependency. But the politics of race is emotionally charged, and differences in opinion and inclination over highly publicized issues are therefore read, by commentators on all sides, as evidence of deep and lasting cleavages.

The image of cleavages, of fissures over race, is a natural one. It is partly right in obvious ways, yet misleading in others, above all in conveying an impression of fixed and unbridgeable divisions. We want therefore to explore, from a new angle, cleavages over racial issues by calling attention to an aspect of American thinking about issues of race that has hitherto escaped attention—the extent to which whites can be induced to change their minds about racial issues.

It is not customary to think of the positions white Americans take on issues of race as pliable, as subject to modification. It is not customary to think of the ordinary American as open to persuasion on issues of race because a snapshot picture of the politics of race as it was a generation ago has become fixed in the minds of commentators on all sides. This picture has become so common that its truth is taken for granted.

TAKING A STAND ON RACE

The ordinary world of politics—the politics of defense appropriations, of mass transit, of foreign aid—is far removed from the center of most citizens' concerns. On many of these issues people can forget entirely the position they once took—even, willy-nilly, declare themselves on a later occasion to favor the very opposite of the position they took on an earlier one. They have given many issues so little attention, the issues have mattered so little to them, that they may never have even formed a genuine attitude toward them, one way or the other. Hence the celebrated problem of "nonattitudes." Caught up in a public opinion interview, many would be embarrassed to confess ignorance, to admit they haven't given an issue serious thought. So they say the first thing that comes to mind. And in the process they can wind up taking a stand on an issue just to cover up their failure to have adopted one in the first place.

Race, in contrast, is alleged to be a red-flag issue: it is necessary only to wave it, to evoke immediate and strong feelings. And given the intensity of the feelings attached to questions of race, no one, absolutely no one, has suggested that, in assessing public opinion on issues of race, there is a problem of nonattitudes. No one has argued that the preferences whites express on issues of race are likely to be, with any frequency, pseudo-preferences—opinions made up on the spot to conceal the fact that people hadn't troubled to give these issues even minimal attention. On the contrary, everyone agrees that not only do whites know where they stand on issues of race, but they have their feet, if not exactly set in cement, then at any rate firmly planted.

Not that whites *on both sides* are believed to have made equally firm, equally uncompromising commitments. On the contrary, many have alleged that proponents of government assistance for blacks suffer a strategic softness of commitment. Thus, a parade of public opinion studies since the 1960s showing an overwhelming majority of Americans to be in favor of the principle of racial equality has given less comfort and assurance than might have been expected. White Americans, many commentators fear, either pretend to a degree of support for racial equality they do not sincerely feel, or support racial equality in a sincere but altogether superficial way: willing perhaps to support racial equality as an abstract principle, but unwilling to back concrete policies aimed at making the principle of racial equality a reality. But even supposing this is true, and no direct evidence of it has been advanced so far, what is being suggested is not that whites who ostensibly support racial equality, when presented with an opportunity to put their ideas to the test, undergo a genuine change of mind, but rather that they are, finally, revealing their true colors.

This argument owes its persuasiveness to the continuing festering of race as an issue in American public life. Race has not faded away as an issue; indeed, in some ways it seems even more enfurled in rancor and bad faith. Whites, many commentators believe and still more fear, do not mean what they say when they say they believe in the principle of racial equality. In turn, this cynicism implies that one side of the argument over race is stronger than public opinion polls would suggest. Consider two people. The first says that he believes in racial equality; the second, that blacks are lazy and won't take advantage of the opportunities open to them. The first person's declaration of good will may well arouse suspicion, but the sincerity of the second, the person who says he dislikes blacks, will not be questioned. And so far as this selective suspicion is justified, there is an asymmetry to the politics of race: supporters of government assistance for blacks will be more weakly, and opponents more strongly, committed to their respective positions.

To what extent are Americans in fact fixed in the positions they take on issues of race, and to what extent can they be persuaded to change their positions in the course of an argument? And is it easier to talk a proponent of government assistance for blacks out of his position than an opponent out of hers—and, supposing a difference exists, when does it most often occur, and why?

REAL POLITICS

Political struggles are commonly viewed as a competition or combat between opposing camps. So viewed, the politics of race often comes down to a contest between two sides, one pressing on behalf of blacks and the other resisting, with the remainder of the public sitting, as it were, on the sidelines. Sports and war may be natural metaphors for politics, but they are misleadingly static—misleading, that is, insofar as they suggest that citizens enlist once and for all on one or the other side of an issue.

Consider citizens' reactions to a proposal to raise local taxes for the benefit of the local school district. The public, at the start of a campaign, could be divided into three camps: supporters of the higher taxes, opponents, and uncommitted. But of course the balance of forces can change in the course of the campaign: the pro camp may grow at the expense of the anti, the anti at the expense of the pro, and both pro and anti may pick up support from the sidelines. Campaign outcomes, after all, are very much a matter of who persuades whom. Real politics—and this includes the politics of race—is dynamic, not static. Majorities are made, and unmade. Civil rights advocates battling Jim Crow and racial segregation did not quit at the outset because the largest part of public opinion was not behind them from the beginning. They understood that the political task was precisely to win more people to their side.

Out of the best intentions—because of the very strength of their desire to ensure that public attention remains concentrated on the problem of race prejudice—many commentators have found it difficult to acknowledge that there is now a *politics* of race, and not simply in the derogatory sense of politics. They have had difficulty acknowledging that ordinary Americans pay significant attention to questions of means and ends in making up their minds about issues of race. It has been easier, and has seemed morally more compelling, to emphasize the stark simplicity of a clean, simple dichotomy between those sympathetic to blacks on the one side and those hostile to them on the other. But as we have repeatedly seen, a single faultline no longer defines disagreements over race; merely because a white opposes one racial policy does not mean that he or she is exceptionally likely to oppose every other. On the contrary, different line-ups and different considerations mark the different agendas of race. The line between racial politics and ordinary politics, however cleanly it could be drawn a generation ago, has at many points been erased, and for two opposing reasons. First, public policies dealing with race are inherently contestable, because each policy joins together a variety of sometimes conflicting ends and means. And second, many racial issues are not as riveting as commentators proclaim them to be: the line between ordinary politics and racial politics, for the average citizen, is often blurred.

The conjunction of both these factors—that racial policies are inherently contestable and that they are, by and large, not exceptional—means that slack is built-in to citizens' opinions about racial policies. Partly, it is built-in because ordinary citizens do not pay close attention to politics generally—including racial politics. Still more fundamentally, slack is built-in because substantial numbers of citizens, even those who have formed a genuine attitude on an issue, do not make an unconditional commitment to it. Some people do commit themselves irretrievably to a position on an issue, but many others are not "for" or "against" without qualification. Their support for a policy may be given, then withdrawn, depending on circumstance. Their political commitments are conditional, contingent—including their commitments about race.

Contrary to the common view that white Americans have their feet set in cement on issues of race, we shall demonstrate that there is a marked pliability in American racial policy preferences—a marked readiness, that is, of citizens to change their position if attention is called to different considerations; white Americans' support for a number of racial policies is given, then withdrawn, depending on circumstance. The pliability of racial policy preferences is a neglected chapter of the largely neglected larger story of the *politics* of race—a politics which, we have shown, takes different forms from one policy agenda to another. As we shall see now, in a most fundamental way white Americans distinguish among issues of race: they are open to persuasion to a striking degree on issues on the social welfare agenda, resistant to a striking degree on issues on the race-conscious agenda.

THE COUNTER-ARGUMENT TECHNIQUE

Our objective is to break away from the practice of characterizing white Americans as either proponents or opponents of assistance for blacks, and instead explore the extent to which their beliefs about race are conditional, contingent. But how, exactly, can the strength of white Americans' commitment to, say, the principle of racial equality be measured?

Following past practice, directly: just ask Americans how strongly they agree (or disagree) with the principle of racial equality. But this is hardly convincing. The whole problem is whether you can take a person at his word when he says that he supports racial equality. So we shall take a different tack. The test of whether people are committed to racial equality, we want to insist, is whether they can be talked out of it easily. Similarly, the test of whether they are committed to opposition is whether they can readily be talked out of it.

Political behavior is social behavior: the people around us take positions on issues partly in response to the positions we take, and we take positions on issues partly in response to the positions they take. The opinions we express about political issues, we express in conversations—responding to the opinions of others, while they in turn respond to ours. The one notorious exception is the public opinion interview itself. Characteristically, a public opinion interview makes an all-out effort to ensure that respondents are *not* pressured to favor one answer over another: the wording of questions, the formatting of response alternatives, the ordering of questions, the mannerisms of interviewers—all are vetted with an eye to eliminating pressure on respondents to give a particular answer, or indeed to give any answer at all. The object is to reduce the impact of the question being asked, and of the person asking it, to zero. In contrast, our objective is to transform the study of public opinion from the monologue of the standard interview to (more nearly) the dialogue of ordinary social interaction.

We want of course to retain the systematic character of opinion measurement, yet introduce the interplay of argument and countervailing considerations. Specifically, we want to explore the extent to which white Americans will give up their position on a racial issue when their attention is called to a competing consideration—to a reason for taking the opposite side of the issue, or for avoiding taking a stand at all. It is important, especially since our concern is the politics of race, to emphasize that our exploration of the pliability of racial policy preferences will take place at two different levels. The first, and our point of departure, is to estimate the likelihood white Americans will change their minds—under pressure—on racial issues. Second, we want to identify the reasons why some people can be talked out of their position on an issue of race and others cannot. Some of these reasons, as we shall demonstrate, apply both to proponents and opponents of policies to assist blacks. But at least for issues on the social welfare agenda we detect an asymmetry, with conservatives who have initially strayed being markedly more likely to return to the fold under pressure than are liberals.

The counter-argument technique was devised to see what happens when political opinions are put under pressure. The technique proceeds in two steps. The first is to determine, through standard questions, which side of a racial issue a person favors. Interviews are conducted over the telephone, with interviewers seated in front of a computer screen and keyboard. They enter the answers of respondents as the interview goes along: for example, if a respondent has taken a position in favor of assisting blacks on a particular issue, a score of 1 would be typed in, while if the respondent had opposed assistance, a score of 2 would be entered. So far, standard operating procedure. What is distinctive about the counter-argument procedure is that once respondents have taken a position, we then try to talk them out of it. Counter-arguments have been prepared in advance, and the very act of entering the respondent's position on the issue into the computer calls up, on the interviewer's screen, the argument prepared against *that* position. The interviewer need then only read the counter-argument and record whether the respondent, after reflection, wants to change his mind or is prepared to stick with his initial position on the issue. Pliability, so conceived, has a specific meaning. It refers to situations in which people can be dislodged from positions they have taken on racial issues by calling their attention directly to a competing consideration.

RATES OF CHANGE

As our specific point of departure we want to focus on the social welfare agenda. All respondents in the Race and Politics Survey were asked:

> Now some statements about issues in society today. Some people think that the government in Washington should increase spending for programs to help blacks. Others feel that blacks should rely only on themselves. Which makes more sense to you? Should the government help improve the positions of blacks, or should they rely only on themselves?

If respondents take the position that spending for blacks should be increased, they are presented with the following counter-argument:

> Would you still feel that way even if government help means people get special treatment just because they are black or would that change your mind?

On the other hand, if they take the position that blacks should rely on themselves, the interviewer says:

> Would you still feel that way even if it means that blacks will continue to be poorer and more often out of work than whites or would that change your mind?

How many are induced to change their minds by this pair of arguments? A striking proportion, as the chart on page 144 shows: more than four in every ten were talked out of their positions on the issue of government spending for blacks by one or the other of these counter-arguments.

This result suggests that the opinions of white Americans on at least some racial issues are strikingly pliable. To determine if this result is an aberration, let us turn to the second example we have at hand of an issue on the social welfare agenda—the issue of government assurance of fair treatment in employment for blacks. Are opinions about government oversight in employment pliable to the same degree that attitudes toward government spending are?

The question on fair treatment ran as follows:

> Some people feel that the government in Washington ought to see to it that blacks get fair treatment in jobs. Others feel that this is not the government's business and it should stay out of it. How do you feel? Should the government in Washington see to it that blacks get fair treatment in jobs or should it stay out of it?

Respondents taking the position that government should see to it that blacks get fair treatment in employment were then asked:

> Would you still feel the same way—even if it means that government will have more say in telling people how to run their lives, or do you think that might change your mind?

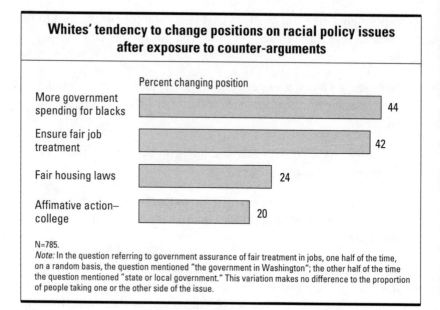

Whites' tendency to change positions on racial policy issues after exposure to counter-arguments

Percent changing position

More government spending for blacks	44
Ensure fair job treatment	42
Fair housing laws	24
Affimative action–college	20

N=785.

Note: In the question referring to government assurance of fair treatment in jobs, one half of the time, on a random basis, the question mentioned "the government in Washington"; the other half of the time the question mentioned "state or local government." This variation makes no difference to the proportion of people taking one or the other side of the issue.

Respondents taking the position that government should stay out of it were asked:

> Would you still feel the same way even if it means that some racial discrimination will continue?

Substantial numbers, again, were willing to give up their position on the issue of fair treatment. Given a gentle nudge in the form of counter-argument, and the counter-arguments amount to no more than a rhetorical nudge, 42 percent of the people change their position on the issue of government assurance of fair treatment in employment, a rate of pliability nearly identical, notwithstanding the quite different counter-arguments deployed, to that observed on the issue of government spending for blacks.

By way of contrast with the social welfare agenda, consider the race-conscious agenda, typified by affirmative action. In assessing people's attitudes, we asked:

> Some people say that because of past discrimination it is sometimes necessary for colleges and universities to reserve openings for black students who don't meet the usual standards. Others are against such quotas. What's your opinion? Are you for or against quotas to admit some black students who don't meet the usual standards?

Following the counter-argument paradigm, having asked respondents to take a position on the issue of affirmative action, we immediately tried to talk them out of it. Specifically, those who favored reserving openings for black students who don't meet the usual standards were asked:

Would you still feel that way, even if it means fewer opportunities for qualified whites, or would you change your mind?

On the other hand, respondents who opposed racial quotas were asked:

Would you still feel that way, even if it means that hardly any blacks would be able to go to the best colleges and universities, or would you change your mind?

The proportion of whites changing their position in consequence of either counter-argument is 20 percent, a pronounced contrast with the pliability of preferences on social welfare issues, which ran double that. These results underline an aspect in which the politics of issues on the social welfare and the race-conscious agenda differ. The positions white Americans take on affirmative action are markedly firmer, less malleable than the positions they take on more traditional forms of government assistance for the disadvantaged.

But what about the third agenda, equal treatment, typified by the issue of fair housing? The issue of residential segregation has been starved of attention. A myriad of studies have been conducted on American attitudes toward busing, or quotas, or government spending in behalf of blacks, but only a handful have been carried out on white Americans' attitudes toward racial integration in housing—a fact that, in itself, speaks to the ironies of the contemporary politics of race.

The issue of whether formally to outlaw racial discrimination in housing is not the same—and is not thought to be the same—as increasing government spending or assigning jobs on the basis of racial quotas. The argument over fair housing is situated against the background of race, but it needs to be understood in its own terms. Drawing on the classic formulation of the General Social

Survey, the issue of fair housing was defined in terms of the following choice:

> Suppose there were a community-wide election on a general housing law and that you had to choose between two possible laws. One law says that homeowners can decide for themselves who to sell their houses to, even if they prefer not to sell to blacks. The second law says that homeowners are not allowed to refuse to sell to someone because of race or color. Which law would you vote for? That homeowners can decide for themselves who to sell to, or that homeowners CAN*NOT* refuse to sell to someone because of race or color?

Respondents who favor homeowners' "rights" were asked:

> Would you feel differently if, as a result of that law, it turned out that blacks were prevented from moving into nice neighborhoods?

Respondents in favor of outlawing racial discrimination in housing were asked:

> Would you feel differently if it turned out that a new government agency had to be set up to enforce that law?

As it turns out, the positions of white Americans on this issue tend to be relatively firm. The rate of pliability—the proportion changing their minds in the face of a counter-argument—is 24 percent, or about one in four.

White Americans, in short, are open to persuasion on some issues of race, much less so on others. The general pattern fits expectations—hardest to dislodge on affirmative action and housing, easiest on issues drawn from the social welfare agenda. The pattern matters, but it is not just the variation across racial issues that matters: as important is the difference in the strength of commitment made by opposing sides on the same issue of race, as we shall now show.

WHICH SIDE CHANGES ITS MIND?

Is it the case, as some suspect and still more fear, that one can talk a white American who supports policies to assist blacks more easily out of her position than one can talk a white American who opposes these policies out of his?

A persisting theme in public commentary on race is that the progress made in building support for the principle of racial equality is superficial. A majority of whites may say they favor the principle of racial equality, but their commitment, it is alleged, is superficial and therefore easily overcome by competing considerations. Not so the views of those whites who are opposed to government action to assure racial equality: they are dug in.

By way of exploring this suggestion of asymmetry, let us begin with a comparison of supporters and opponents of government assistance for blacks of a standard social welfare variety. As the chart on page 148 shows, the probability of giving up a "problack" position under pressure is greater than that of giving up an "antiblack" position. Consider first the issue of increased government spending to assist blacks: 52 percent of people supporting such an increase in government spending change their minds, given the opportunity for second thought, as compared with 40 percent of people opposing such an increase. These figures suggest that it is easier—not immensely but significantly easier—to talk a proponent of government assistance for blacks out of his position than an opponent out of hers.

One might argue, however, that this difference reflects not the weakness of the commitment of proponents of government spending for blacks to their position but rather the strength of the particular counter-argument directed against their position. But to put the issue this way misses the point. The counter-arguments deployed in the course of the interview are in fact the natural arguments that tend to be made against particular positions in real life. And what we want to get some sense of, even if only approximately, is the fate of particular positions if people are caught up in the hurly-burly of actual argumentation.

This is not to suggest that the counter-arguments that were deployed are the only ones that could conceivably have been put in play. And indeed, precisely to sample the competing considerations which can be evoked, different counter-arguments were deployed, on both sides. So, in trying to dislodge people from a "problack" position on the two social welfare questions, we brought up the problem of special treatment in one case and the risk of government having more power in telling people how to run their lives in the other; and in trying to dislodge people from an "antiblack" position, we mentioned the problem of black

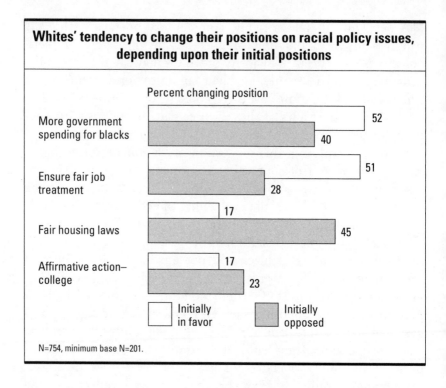

Whites' tendency to change their positions on racial policy issues, depending upon their initial positions

Percent changing position

More government spending for blacks
- 52 (Initially in favor)
- 40 (Initially opposed)

Ensure fair job treatment
- 51 (Initially in favor)
- 28 (Initially opposed)

Fair housing laws
- 17 (Initially in favor)
- 45 (Initially opposed)

Affirmative action— college
- 17 (Initially in favor)
- 23 (Initially opposed)

☐ Initially in favor   ▨ Initially opposed

N=754, minimum base N=201.

poverty in one case, and the persistence of racial discrimination in the other. The hypothesis of asymmetry in the pliability of positions on social welfare policies would be strengthened substantially if we were to find the same pattern of results for the issue of government assurance of fair treatment in employment as for government spending.

What we found, as the chart shows, was even stronger evidence of asymmetry: 51 percent of the proponents of government assurances of fair treatment—one in every two—changed their minds if fair treatment means that government will have more say in telling people how to run their lives; on the other side of the issue, only 28 percent of those who opposed government assurances of fair treatment in employment for blacks were willing to change their minds *even* if the absence of such assurances means the persistence of racial discrimination.

The politics of affirmative action, though, has a different temper than the politics of social welfare, and this difference in temper should show up in the readiness of whites to hold their ground on an issue like affirmative action. The question of quotas and preferential treatment engages people's fundamental beliefs about fairness—on both sides of the issue of affirmative action. The positions whites take on it should be more firmly held, should represent more unconditional commitments than the positions they take on an issue like government spending—and symmetrically so. It should, it follows, be difficult to dislodge an opponent of affirmative action from her position—*and* a supporter from his. And this is what we found: as the chart shows, only 17 percent of proponents of affirmative action can be talked out of their position by the counter-argument, and only 23 percent of opponents out of theirs.

This approximate parity on opposite sides of the issue in the case of affirmative action highlights an aspect of the politics of race easily misconstrued. It is a part of political folklore to suppose that people who take the minority position on a salient issue have more intense preferences than those on the majority side—after all, their minority position is itself proof of their readiness to resist the majority point of view. And insofar as the preferences of a minority are more intense, they should adhere to them more tenaciously. Political folklore, moreover, corresponds to social-psychological theory. The fewer the people who agree with a person, the more likely is that person to encounter arguments against her position. And the more practice she has had in defending her position, the argument runs, the more resistant she should be to persuasion, other things equal. Hence, people who take the minority side of a contested political issue should be more resistant to persuasion than those who take the majority side.

Is a majority, just by virtue of being a majority, inherently more vulnerable to counter-pressures? In the Bay Area nearly three in every four respondents—a clear majority—favor a law against discrimination in the sale of houses. Are these proponents of fair housing easier to talk out of their position than are opponents out of theirs? In fact, as the chart shows, whites on the *un*popular, not the popular, side of the issue are more pliable: of those who oppose fair housing, nearly one in every two change their minds after exposure to a counter-argument; among proponents of fair housing, only one in every six.

These results thus teach a double lesson. First, a minority is not inherently more firmly committed to its position on an issue than an issue majority. Opponents of affirmative action—overwhelmingly, the majority in the public as a whole—are as hard to dislodge from their positions on the issue as proponents of it. And proponents of fair housing—also the majority position—are harder to dislodge from their position on the issue than are opponents. Second, and in consequence, patterns of pliability vary from one racial agenda to another. Supporters of social welfare policies to benefit blacks are easier to talk out of their positions than opponents. But opponents are easier than supporters to talk out of their position on the issue of fair housing.

SOME THOUGHT EXPERIMENTS

The meaning we give to politics at any one moment depends partly on our judgments about whether it is frozen in place, at any rate over the immediate prospect, or open to change. Perhaps the most important consideration in determining whether the politics of race is open to change, though not the only one, is the stability of popular majorities on issues of race. Consider first opinions about the social welfare agenda, beginning with the issue of government spending to assist blacks. A majority of whites in the Bay Area support increasing the amount of money government spends to assist blacks, as we have seen. What, we want to ask, is the fate of this majority if whites are subjected to pressure to change their minds? Would there still be a majority in favor of social welfare policies to help blacks if people on both sides of the issue were exposed to arguments against the position they are initially inclined to take? Will problack majorities dissolve if proponents and opponents of government assistance are equally likely to run into arguments that might cause them to reconsider their position?

The pie charts on page 151—one pair for each of four racial issues—contrast two situations: first, when no pressure on either side of the issue is exerted, and second, when arguments are made on both sides of the issue. In the case of more government spending for blacks, when there is no pressure to favor either side, a majority of 57 percent favors more government help for blacks. However, where there is pressure both in favor of and in opposition to increased government spending for blacks, there is now a 56 percent majority on the *opposite* side of the issue, in favor of the

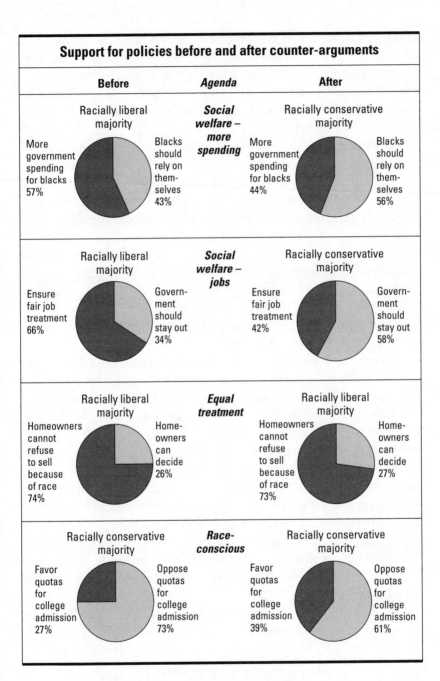

Support for policies before and after counter-arguments

Before	Agenda	After

Racially liberal majority
Social welfare – more spending
Racially conservative majority

More government spending for blacks 57%

Blacks should rely on themselves 43%

More government spending for blacks 44%

Blacks should rely on themselves 56%

Racially liberal majority
Social welfare – jobs
Racially conservative majority

Ensure fair job treatment 66%

Government should stay out 34%

Ensure fair job treatment 42%

Government should stay out 58%

Racially liberal majority
Equal treatment
Racially liberal majority

Homeowners cannot refuse to sell because of race 74%

Homeowners can decide 26%

Homeowners cannot refuse to sell because of race 73%

Homeowners can decide 27%

Racially conservative majority
Race-conscious
Racially conservative majority

Favor quotas for college admission 27%

Oppose quotas for college admission 73%

Favor quotas for college admission 39%

Oppose quotas for college admission 61%

idea that blacks should take care of their own problems rather than rely on the government. What does this indicate about the stability of policy majorities on issues of race? It suggests that pro-black majorities can be vulnerable. They can be replaced by counter-majorities if attention is drawn, on an equal basis, to competing considerations.

The results of a comparable thought experiment for the issue of government assurance of fair treatment in employment for blacks perfectly parallels that for increased governmental spending, as the second pair of pie charts show. Again, a majority in favor of increased government assistance for blacks, absent pressure, gives way to a majority opposed to more government assistance when pressure on *both* sides is exerted. And the parallelism of results on these two issues suggests that the current majority in favor of government activism to assist blacks harbors within it a counter-majority—a counter-majority that is more likely to emerge the more attention is given to strong arguments both for and against social welfare assistance for blacks.

In contrast, the majorities on affirmative action and fair housing are markedly more stable. Primarily, that is because of the size of the initial majorities—in opposition to the former and in favor of the latter. But partly it is because one side of the issue seems to be easier to talk out of its position, though further tests are necessary before firm conclusions can be drawn.

But *why* can some people can be talked out of their position by a counter-argument while others cannot? Reasons for giving up a position on an issue fall into two classes: symmetrical reasons—factors that work to induce people to change their position on a racial issue regardless of the stand they take; and asymmetrical reasons—factors that work to make it easier, on any given issue of race, to change the minds of people on one side of the issue rather than on the other.

We shall start with symmetrical forms of issue pliability, then turn to asymmetrical ones.

NONATTITUDES AND PERSUASIBILITY

Why are some people—whether they have chosen to support or oppose government policies to assist blacks—easier to dislodge from their position on a racial issue than others? We want to focus on two kinds of symmetrical reasons—nonattitudes and persuasibility.

Measuring the extent to which ordinary citizens changed their positions on policy issues, Philip Converse (1970) demonstrated that the probability of ordinary citizens' taking the same side of a public issue, over two-year intervals, is depressingly low, and their attitudes were not markedly more stable over a two-year interval than over a six-year stretch. Piqued by this oddity—since ordinarily one would expect political attitudes to be more stable, other things equal, the shorter the period of time involved—Converse devised the "black-and-white" model of change. He calculated rates of change, issue by issue, on the assumption that respondents were either perfectly stable or chose their position altogether randomly—hence the expression "black-and-white" model. The empirical results, though varying from issue to issue, were dramatic, for they plainly implied that the majority of people take a position, on at least one issue, as though they are flipping a coin.

The notion that large numbers of people pick their positions on political issues randomly may seem at first bizarre. Yet, the nonattitudes hypothesis owes its persuasiveness in large part to the explanation that Converse offered for randomness in response. As he suggested, "It seems to me most simple to imagine that [such random responses] came from people with no real attitudes on the matter in question, but who for some reason felt obliged to try a response to the item despite our generous and repeated invitation to disavow any opinion where one was not felt."

This is, psychologically, a shrewd thrust. For the public opinion interview sets up its own expectations and standards of evaluation, notwithstanding the overall effort to put respondents at ease. Frequently, a person being interviewed finds the attention flattering: here is somebody who actually wishes to know what *he* thinks about key issues of public policy, by no means an everyday experience for everyone. But a failure to be able to answer anything at all can be demeaning. To answer, "I don't know," "I haven't thought about that," "I haven't paid attention" to question after question may stamp one as embarrassingly ignorant or inexcusably indifferent to one's responsibilities as a citizen. And how better to conceal the fact that no position has been taken than to express one—any one. Hence the expression "nonattitudes."

A nontrivial number of citizens express nonattitudes when asked their position on a political issue. But it has never been suggested that this behavior applies to issues of race. On the contrary, it has seemed obvious that issues of race evoke strong emotional reactions, and this implies that ordinary citizens can hardly be making up their views on issues of race on the spot, to disguise the fact that they hadn't given the issues much thought.

The most important thing to appreciate about the thinking of whites on race, we now believe, is that many of them do not very often think about it at all. For all the attention given to the problem of malice, which a nontrivial number of whites surely feel for blacks, scarcely any thought has been given to the problem of sheer indifference, which is characteristic of far more whites. But there are good reasons why whites might not make the issue of race central to their concerns. They neither suffer directly from the problem of racial inequality, nor see themselves as directly responsible for it. The problem of race is, like many other problems of public policy, a secondary concern in the daily lives of whites and of only occasional interest to them.

Once the fact of white indifference or detachment is borne in mind, it can be seen that racial issues are more akin to the ordinary run of political issues than has hitherto been recognized. Thus, rather than changing their minds in the face of a counter-argument, perhaps many whites never had them made up in the first place. Racial policy preferences may be, in significant measure, nonattitudes.

How can this be shown empirically? Take the issue of government assistance for blacks. We know from previous research that people have in mind a pair of considerations when they take a stand on social welfare issues. One of these is their overall orientation to government—their ideology. A person who is broadly liberal in political outlook will tend to favor such assistance to blacks; in contrast, one who is conservative will tend to oppose it. Another consideration they typically have in mind is how they feel toward blacks: not surprisingly, the more negative a person's feelings toward blacks, the more likely he is to oppose the government's giving them help, while conversely, the more positive a person's feelings toward blacks, the more likely he is to support such help being provided blacks. With this in mind, it is possible to establish a test of the nonattitudes argument by taking advantage of the counter-argument paradigm.

Think of the public as a whole as made of two parts. One part consists of people who had a relevant reason in mind (such as ideological orientation or feelings about blacks) for taking a position on the issue of government assistance for blacks. The other part consists of people who took a position on the issue not because they had worked through the implications of either their overall outlook on politics or their orientation toward blacks, but instead because they felt that they should say something—anything—about the issue. We would expect that the people who change their position on an issue of race would turn out to be the very same people who did not have a good reason for taking the position they did in the first place.

If our reasoning is right, it should be relatively easy to predict the original position of whites who resist a counter-argument—the "stayers"—if we know how liberal or conservative they perceive themselves to be and whether they perceive blacks to be making a genuine effort. On the other hand, it should be quite difficult to predict the position of whites who give in to a counter-argument—the "movers"—even if we know exactly the same things about them.

As the chart on page 156 shows, the contrast between stayers and movers is striking. On the issue of whether government spending in behalf of blacks should be increased, we found the positions of stayers to be highly predictable. On the other hand, the positions of movers were barely predictable above and beyond chance, suggesting that those who changed their position on the issue of race after hearing a counter-argument tended to be people who hadn't acted on a relevant reason for taking it in the first place. We found the same pattern to hold true for the issue of whether government should attempt to assure fair treatment in employment for blacks.

To sum up, the results of two independent tests of the nonattitudes hypothesis point in exactly the same direction. People who can be talked out of their position on an issue of race tend to share a telltale characteristic. They tend *not* to have had a consistent

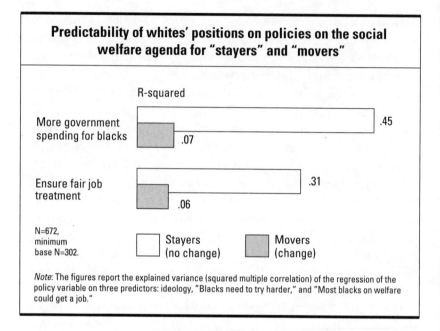

Predictability of whites' positions on policies on the social welfare agenda for "stayers" and "movers"

R-squared

More government spending for blacks
.45
.07

Ensure fair job treatment
.31
.06

N=672, minimum base N=302.

☐ Stayers (no change)   ▨ Movers (change)

Note: The figures report the explained variance (squared multiple correlation) of the regression of the policy variable on three predictors: ideology, "Blacks need to try harder," and "Most blacks on welfare could get a job."

reason for taking the position they did in the first place. And this throws new light on the thinking of whites about issues of race. For it makes plain that their levels of attention toward and investment in the positions they take, if not on all issues of race then on a number of key ones, are of a piece with their thinking about political issues in general. The politics of race belongs to ordinary politics, to a degree not appreciated by either proponents or opponents of government assistance for blacks.

Quite apart from the issue of nonattitudes, though, is the question of persuasibility. If a person had not genuinely taken a position on an issue, then it cannot strictly be right to say that he has been persuaded to change his mind. But surely some of the time people are induced to change their mind by a counter-argument because they have undergone a process of persuasion. The term "persuasion" covers a lot of territory. In particular, we want to be agnostic with respect to time. The effects of counter-arguments may be enduring, though we suspect not. But whether permanent or transient, what is politically relevant is the fact that substantial numbers of people can be induced to abandon positions they have taken on issues of race, given only the gentle nudge of a counter-argument; and so what we want to understand is what distinguishes those people who can be easily induced to defect from those who cannot. By persuasion, then, we mean (roughly) a readiness to yield a position on one side of an issue, though not necessarily to adopt one on the other, in response to a counter-argument. And what we want to suggest is that the reason some people are persuaded is because they are inherently persuasible—and would have yielded to whatever particular counter-argument was directed against them.

Intuitively, we all know some person whose positions on political issues depend very much on where he is and who he is with: he will tinge his opinions with a pleasingly liberal tincture when the people he wishes to please are liberal, or paint them in flatteringly conservative tones when the people he wants to please are conservative. The point to appreciate about the person who is persuasible is that he is *indiscriminately* so. This intuition that some people are indiscriminately open to influence is very much at the center of the notion of persuasibility that we want to explore here.

The persuasibility hypothesis and the nonattitudes hypothesis, although bearing a family resemblance, are more akin to second cousins than to blood brothers. And the best way to distinguish them is to distinguish between "topic-free" and "topic-bound" susceptibility to influence. A topic-bound susceptibility "is always limited to one class of communications (a narrow or a broad class) which is defined by one or another characteristic of the content of the conclusion." In contrast, topic-free susceptibility refers to a susceptibility to influence which is "relatively free of the subject matter of the communication." Nonattitudes are always topic-bound, since the whole point is that a person's response to an issue is pliable just insofar as *that* issue has not seriously engaged his interest and hence he has not formed a genuine attitude about it. In contrast, persuasibility is topic-free: some people can be dislodged from their positions on political issues pretty much across-the-board, by pretty much any plausible counter-argument. The person who is persuasible with respect to issue X should tend to be persuasible with respect to issue Y; and the person who finds counter-argument A persuasive because he is persuasible should tend to find counter-argument B persuasive, too. This double susceptibility—across issues and across counter-arguments—implies that the person who changes his position after hearing a counter-argument did so because he was vulnerable not to a specially crafted and singularly appropriate counter-argument but to counter-argumentation *per se*.

If the heart of the matter is vulnerability to counter-argumentation and not a particular counter-argument, an appropriate testing procedure suggests itself. The nub of the procedure is this. Respondents are exposed to counter-arguments on four issues. To determine whether some of them changed their mind about a particular issue simply because they were persuasible, count the number of times that they changed their minds on the other three issues, disregarding completely the content of these issues and of the specific counter-arguments used in conjunction with them. If the persuasibility hypothesis holds, then the more often people were induced to change their mind on other issues, the more likely they should have been to change their mind about the first issue.

Consider, first, people whose initial position is to support increased government spending for blacks. Suppose they are sorted out according to how often they have changed their mind on other issues in the face of a counter-argument, from those who have maintained their position in all circumstances to those who have given it up in all. As the chart on page 159 shows, we found a clear connection between the probability of their changing their positions on a given issue and the frequency of their having changed positions on others. For example, people who had changed their positions on either two or three of the other racial issues were overwhelmingly likely to change their position on the issue of government spending—to be exact, 63 percent of the former, and 74 percent of the latter, changed their minds in the face of a counter-argument. In contrast, those who declined to change their position on any of the other occasions were overwhelmingly likely to decline to change their position on government spending—more than two thirds of them holding their position notwithstanding the counter-argument.

The same is true for the issue of the government's ensuring fair treatment: people who changed their position on other racial issues in the face of a counter-argument tended to be the ones who changed their position on this issue when given a comparable nudge. In short, it is not that people who change their minds on

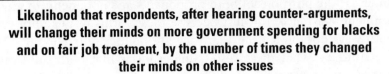

Likelihood that respondents, after hearing counter-arguments, will change their minds on more government spending for blacks and on fair job treatment, by the number of times they changed their minds on other issues

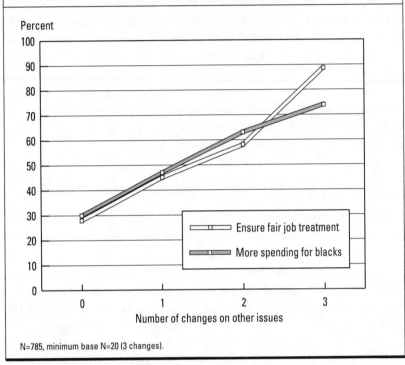

N=785, minimum base N=20 (3 changes).

government oversight do so because they were vulnerable to the specific counter-arguments deployed. On the contrary, they tend to be the very same people who changed on other issues when quite different counter-arguments were employed.

To sum up, we have located so far a pair of explanations for the pliability of racial policy preferences—the nonattitudes hypothesis, which suggests that the reason people are amenable to changing their minds is because they haven't really made it up in the first place, and the persuasibility hypothesis, which holds that people give way in the face of counter-arguments not because particular arguments are specifically compelling to them but because they are vulnerable to counter-argumentation *per se*. Both explanations, we would emphasize, apply *symmetrically*—that is, they undercut the positions of both proponents and opponents of government assistance. But just because these forms of pliability cut both ways does not mean that they are politically irrelevant. On the contrary, what these results underline is that both sides can increase their strength merely by drawing from the ranks of those on the other side who have nonattitudes or are persuasible. If politics consists in strategic efforts either to cut into the strength of the opponent's position or bolster one's own, there is, these results make plain, built-in room for maneuver.

What we want to consider now is whether one or the other side of the issue of race operates under a special handicap. Is it easier to talk proponents of government assistance for blacks out of their position than opponents out of theirs?

IDEOLOGY AND ANTIBLACK FEELINGS

The question of asymmetry in the politics of race is crucial because it goes to the politically strategic question of whether one side of the issue has an advantage over the other.

From the results we have seen thus far, it hardly makes sense to suppose that a proponent of affirmative action is distinctly easier to talk out of his position than an opponent is out of hers, and if either side is more vulnerable on the issue of fair housing, it is opponents, not proponents. On the other hand, we have seen that there is good reason to suppose that proponents of social welfare assistance for blacks are easier to talk out of their positions than opponents are out of theirs. Accordingly, in exploring for asymmetries in racial politics, we shall concentrate on the politics of the social welfare agenda.

The crucial feature to focus on is the phenomenon of loose linkages. Issues on the social welfare agenda, as we have observed, have a definite ideological component. For perfectly obvious reasons, a proposal to increase government spending for blacks is more likely to appeal to a political liberal, less likely to appeal to a political conservative. Thus, the correlation between the positions whites take on the issue of increasing government spending for blacks and their ideological self-identification and feelings toward blacks is sizeable. But it is far from perfect. A fair number of people who think of themselves as conservative nonetheless express initial support for more government spending to assist blacks, while a sizeable number who think of themselves as liberal nonetheless take the position that blacks should take care of their problems on their own. There are, then, inevitably mixed coalitions on both sides of the issue of government spending for blacks, with each side of the issue commanding the initial support of the bulk of its "partisans" admixed with a sizeable number of "defectors" from the other side. And this makes perfectly good sense. Why would one expect ordinary citizens, who pay only intermittent attention to politics, always to line up on the "right" side, as though they were soldiers on parade? On the contrary, the linkage between ideology and issue position is—and ought to be—discernibly loose.

But suppose an effort is made to tighten up the linkages between ideological orientation and issue preference, which is, after all, what the process of political persuasion and argumentation aims at. Are liberals who initially have opposed government assistance for blacks as likely to return to their ideological home as are conservatives who have supported government assistance?

The conservative who has initially taken a liberal position on the issue of government spending, we want to suggest, is more likely to return to the fold, if exposed to an appeal to do so, than will the liberal who has taken a conservative position on the issue. Why this difference? From a strictly logical perspective, the conservative who has taken a liberal position on the issue of government spending for blacks and the liberal who has taken a racially conservative position on the same issue are in the same position: each has departed from his or her overall political orientation. But if their position is the same logically, it is not at all the same politically.

Consider the conservative who, asked her position on increasing government spending for blacks, takes the liberal side of the issue. She has gone out of her way. She has demonstrated compassion and generosity. She has shown that she is not tainted with race prejudice. And having shown all this, she is free to return to a conservative position when the counter-argument supplies her an opportunity for reconsideration. Contrast this with the liberal who has taken a racially conservative position on the issue of government spending. He is being asked to stand behind a familiar, mainstream liberal proposition, not a new and especially controversial policy like affirmative action. It is telling when a liberal cannot bring himself to support so familiar and central a plank in his political platform. Accordingly, it should be harder to persuade a liberal who has taken a racially conservative stand to return to the fold than to persuade a conservative who has taken a racially liberal stand to come home.

The argument on asymmetry goes beyond ideology. Consider the other principal factor underpinning the positions Americans take on racial welfare issues—how they feel about blacks—and focus first on the white who initially supports more government assistance for blacks notwithstanding his negative feelings toward them. Having shown his compassion and freedom from prejudice, he is free to accept an invitation to reconsider his views and return to a position he more naturally favors. Now, consider the person with positive feelings toward blacks and who nonetheless takes the position that they should take care of their problems on their own. Given her positive feelings toward blacks, it should have been easy for her to favor government help for them. And the fact that she did not bespeaks a strong motivation. And given that she was strongly motivated to say that blacks should deal with their problems by themselves, she would *a fortiori* be difficult to dislodge from this position.

The argument, then, is that there is a *causal* asymmetry. Ideology and feelings about blacks are potent forces in organizing the reactions of whites to social welfare issues. But they are not equally potent in ensuring that people, having selected a position on an issue of race, will stick to it in the face of pressure to change. To determine whether this causal asymmetry holds or not, a series of tests were performed. The first of these shows the relation between people's ideological self-identification and the likelihood of changing their mind in the face of a counter-argument, depending on whether their initial preference was to favor or to oppose increased government spending for blacks. Examining respondents initially supporting increased spending for blacks first, we can see a marked relationship between their ideological orientation and the probability of their changing their mind in the face of a counter-argument. As the chart on page 163 shows, only conservatives (and to a lesser degree moderates) who have taken a

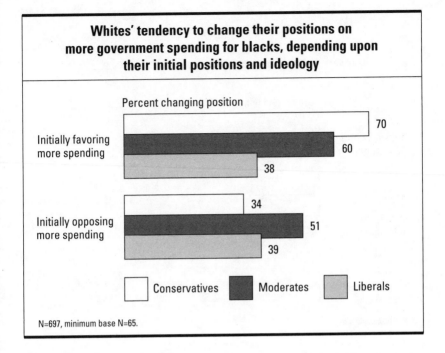

Whites' tendency to change their positions on more government spending for blacks, depending upon their initial positions and ideology

Percent changing position

Initially favoring more spending
- 70
- 60
- 38

Initially opposing more spending
- 34
- 51
- 39

☐ Conservatives ■ Moderates ▨ Liberals

N=697, minimum base N=65.

liberal position on the issue of government spending are overwhelmingly likely to return to their political home following an appeal to their overall political point of view. Specifically, 70 percent of conservatives who have taken a liberal position on government spending change their mind in the face of a counter-argument. In contrast, white liberals who have taken a conservative position on the issue are not in any significant degree more likely to switch to a liberal position than are white conservatives who have taken a conservative position. It is thus easier to get conservatives than liberals who have defected on a racial issue to return to their ideological home.

This ideological asymmetry is part, we suspect, of a broader asymmetry. Consider the relation between people's feelings toward blacks and the probability they will change their minds on a social welfare issue if exposed to a counter-argument. Looking first at people whose initial response is favorable to government assistance for blacks, we see in the chart on page 164 that the more they perceive blacks to be failing to make a genuine effort to deal with their problems, the more likely they are—in the face of a

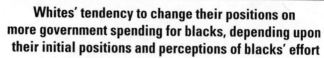

Whites' tendency to change their positions on more government spending for blacks, depending upon their initial positions and perceptions of blacks' effort

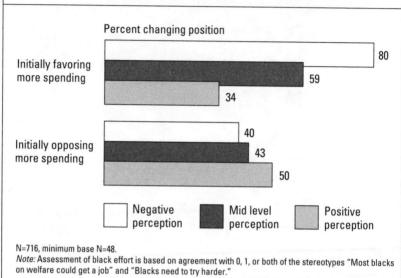

Percent changing position

Initially favoring more spending
- 80
- 59
- 34

Initially opposing more spending
- 40
- 43
- 50

☐ Negative perception   ■ Mid level perception   ☐ Positive perception

N=716, minimum base N=48.
Note: Assessment of black effort is based on agreement with 0, 1, or both of the stereotypes "Most blacks on welfare could get a job" and "Blacks need to try harder."

counter-argument—to give up their initial support for blacks and to say that they have changed their minds. Of those who tend to see blacks in this light, 80 percent gave up their support for increasing spending to assist blacks after hearing a counter-argument, compared with only 34 percent of those with a markedly more positive evaluation of blacks. However, the reverse is not true on the other side of the issue. Perceiving blacks as making an effort to improve their lot is *not* associated with a comparable increase in the likelihood of defecting from a racially conservative position on social welfare issues. Simply put, those who like blacks are not significantly more likely to surrender their opposition to government assistance—even in the face of an explicit appeal to give consideration to the well-being of blacks—than are those who dislike blacks. This same pattern holds for the fair jobs question.

All these results add up to an invitation to take seriously the possibility that the politics of social welfare issues is characterized by systematic asymmetries in the inclination of people to change their minds. We are not contending that underlying causal factors favor the same side on every issue of race. On the contrary, we have seen that it is easier to talk opponents of fair housing out of their position than proponents out of theirs. But having said this, we are persuaded that an asymmetry in pliability for an important class of racial issues—those on the social welfare agenda—exists. When push comes to shove, advocates of more social welfare assistance for blacks have a harder time holding on to their coalition than do advocates of black self-help.

A FINAL WORD

Our specific findings to one side, we want to underline our general theme. It has been common, indeed more or less unchallenged, to speak of racial politics as though it was static, with whites fixed in place, often by virtue of their early upbringing. But the point precisely in emphasizing a politics of race is to highlight the potential for change—for movement and counter-movement. Many citizens are fixed in place on issues of race, and on some issues of race—above all, on affirmative action, preferences are so one-sided as to seem irreversible. But on the largest number of racial issues, non-trivial numbers of whites are open to persuasion. New majorities can be made—and unmade. The future is not foreordained. It is the business of politics to decide it.

CONCLUSION: IRONIES

Vagueness is the past's advantage over the present. The anger and resentment that overhang the contemporary politics of race invite a tendency to look back, to remember a contrasting moment—say, when hundreds of thousands of men and women, white and black, marched up Pennsylvania Avenue to listen to King tell of a dream, and much, if not everything, seemed possible. But nostalgia is a snare: the momentous Civil Rights Acts of 1964 and 1965 went arm in arm with the devastating riots in Watts and Detroit.

It is hard to get the balance of past and present right, yet it is manifest that the optimism born of the civil rights movement of the 1960s has long since died. Cynicism and resentment on all sides have taken its place, fed by more than one source but swollen by one fundamental error: the equation of whites' attitudes toward public policies dealing with blacks with their attitudes toward blacks themselves. Making this fundamental mistake has been misleading twice over. On the one side, it has encouraged an impression that the nature of racial *prejudice* has changed, although it has not, and on the other side, it has reinforced a conviction that the shape of racial *politics* has not changed, even though it has.

To begin with the nature of prejudice, the historic changes in the politics of race in the 1960s suggested to a generation of researchers that racial bigotry had lost its place in American life. No one supposed that the disappearance of the public symbols of racism meant that racial prejudice itself had disappeared. But the traditional forms of bigotry—with their open and unqualified declaration of the intellectual and moral inferiority of blacks—had lost their public props and public respectability with the collapse of *de jure* segregation. The bigot, it seemed to follow, would now be self-conscious, unsure of his ground, aware at a minimum that the ideas and feelings he clung to about blacks violated the new standards of social acceptability, concerned therefore to hide—certainly from a stranger's eyes—the race prejudice he still harbored. The bigot had, in his own eyes, lost his place in American society.

This view of prejudice, although part and parcel of a larger argument meant to warn of the continuing dangers of racism, ironically exaggerates the weakness of prejudice. In fact, race prejudice owes its strength to the fact that, from the point of view of the person who subscribes to it, it is not prejudice at all. The racial bigot does not see *himself* as a bigot, merely as a person who sees blacks as they are, for what they are; and there is nothing he has to be ashamed about just because blacks (in his eyes) have much about which to be ashamed. The failings are theirs, not his. To suppose that a controlling desire of racists is to hide their racism is to misread racism altogether.

Bigotry *has* given ground. But because some racial stereotypes have passed out of fashion—because relatively few whites continue to parrot that blacks are born inferior—does not mean that the nature of racial prejudice has changed. It remains the same compound of malignancy and ignorance notwithstanding the repeated pronouncements of the demise of old-fashioned bigotry. How can one tell that today's racial prejudice is at its core the same as the prejudice of a generation ago? Because now, just as before, hostility and resentment and contempt for blacks are part and parcel of a broader ethnocentric outlook. By way of showing this, we have demonstrated the powerful covariation between agreement with negative stereotypes of blacks and agreement with negative stereotypes of Jews. Believe that blacks are irresponsible, dangerous, lazy and the chances are excellent that you will believe that Jews are unscrupulous and untrustworthy—and vice versa. The interknittedness of stereotypes of blacks and Jews testifies to the tenacity of racial prejudice. A half century ago, Jews were at the margins of American society, conspicuously disadvantaged, if not so viciously as blacks. Now, Jews as a group score as high above the norm in material success as blacks have scored below; Jews also differ from blacks in the probability of keeping the family intact, doing well in education, and staying within the law—all measures used to justify negative characterizations of blacks. But all of these differences in the objective circumstances of blacks and Jews notwithstanding, both are bound up in a common fate, common victims of an unreasoning aversion to others whose appearance or background or religion or manners differ from the majority. These findings remind us that it is not the actual characteristics of blacks, any more than it is the actual characteristics of Jews, that evoke the root prejudice against both. It is the fact of their difference, in and of itself, that renders them vulnerable. Our results thus point to the persistence of fundamental irrationality at the core of prejudice, now as much as ever.

Recognizing that there are fewer bigots now than a generation ago, most whites insist that racial discrimination, if it has not completely disappeared, has been largely erased. On the other side, recognizing that racial inequality has by no means been eradicated, most blacks insist that racial discrimination persists. And in between, thoughtful Americans, black or white, tend to be caught in a clash of intuitions—that much has improved and that the problem nonetheless persists.

To what extent does racial discrimination in fact endure? Honoring a claim to a public benefit or governmental service, if made by a white, but refusing to honor exactly the same claim if made by a black, *is* discrimination; and our findings on racial double standards—made possible for the first time by new methods—point to a central paradox of racial discrimination in contemporary American life. On the one side, when it comes to judgments about public benefits that should be provided to *individual* citizens, there is no racial double standard. In the "laid-off worker" experiment, whites were evenhanded in judgments of claims to public benefits:

they were just as likely to believe that the government should help a black who has lost a job find a new one as a white who has been laid off. It would be a mistake, of course, to take the results of one experiment and conclude that there is no longer significant racial discrimination at any level, still more of a mistake to take the results from an experiment conducted in only one part of the country and apply it without qualification to the country as a whole. Still, the results of the laid-off worker experiment speak to a sea change since midcentury, when racial double standards were an open and legitimate feature of American life. Evenhandedness in honoring claims to government assistance made by particular individuals regardless of their race is one face of the issue of race in contemporary American life, a face that advertises the progress made over the last four decades.

But the issue of race has another face—every bit as real as the first. The "equal opportunity" experiment framed the problem of discrimination at a different level than did the laid-off worker experiment. The crux of the issue was the handling of claims not of specific individuals but rather of groups—a matter not of whether to honor a claim to government assistance of this particular person who among other things is a black, but instead whether to honor a claim to equal opportunity of blacks as a *group* to government assistance. The evenhandedness characteristic of reactions to blacks as individuals is not characteristic of reactions to blacks as a group. We found significantly more support for government guarantees of equal opportunity for women than for blacks.

The results of the two experiments thus point in opposite directions—the laid-off worker experiment demonstrating an absence of a racial double standard, the equal opportunity experiment illustrating the persistence of one. But it would be a mistake to view these findings as contradicting each other. Both findings—of fairness and of bias—are valid. The difference between the two follows from the larger role of stereotypes in judgments of blacks as a group rather than blacks as individuals. It would be captious to insist that judgment at one level, individual or group, is somehow more real than the other. But the kinds of political judgments that ordinary citizens are asked to make are very much more often judgments about what ought to be done in behalf of blacks *taken as a group*, and only incidentally and occasionally about individual blacks.

What factors work against this kind of racial discrimination? The first generation of systematic studies of prejudice saw the educational system as a prime social institution combatting prejudice. Prejudice, according to the classical studies, was a subset of a larger set of ideas—ideas that are simplistic, overly generalized, at odds with the dominant values of the official culture in American life. And the greater the opportunity ordinary citizens have had for formal education, the more developed their skills in inference and critical thinking, the more extensive and thorough their exposure to the values of democracy, tolerance, and rationality at the heart of the American ethos, the more consistently and intimately associated they are with others who are also well educated and provide social support for the norm of tolerance—or at any rate, social sanctions for deviation from it.

This argument on the connection between educational opportunity and tolerance, though made on empirical and quantitative grounds, gave renewed strength to a prominent strand of American thought on the moral foundations of democracy, a strand epitomized by the liberal pragmatism of the philosopher and educator John Dewey. Dewey argued powerfully in behalf of the idea that ordinary citizens, partly by participation in public affairs but as much through education, could equip themselves to play a responsible role in democratic politics. Dewey's conviction about the potential of ordinary people, a potential that could and would be realized by a liberal education, gave a dignity to ordinary citizens they had historically been denied. Rather than being represented as free riders, making their chief contribution by their indifference and abstention from an active role in the deliberation of public affairs, citizens were seen as having the potential to strengthen their own commitment to democratic values, and in the process to strengthen the sway of democratic values over the conduct of public business.

The years since the climax of the civil rights movement have seen an enveloping cynicism about the institutions of American society, and this has most certainly included the educational system. Perhaps a reaction was inevitable; but with an irony that is unmistakable, it has taken the form of questioning the very institution liberals used to celebrate. What comes with the opportunity for higher education, it is now claimed, is not the genuine learning of the values of the culture but rather the shrewdness to simulate them. The better educated are not more tolerant racially or politically, merely more deft at impression management, more adept at portraying themselves as believing and in the habit of doing what a good citizen ought to believe and do. Education, the argument runs, has little to do with doing the right thing—but a lot to do with saying the right thing.

Is education, as Dewey and others have maintained, a mainstay of democratic values, including racial tolerance, or is its influence, as more recent commentators have suggested, chiefly confined to the teaching of manners? Ironically, the very depth of current cynicism about the role of education has stymied efforts to investigate the issue. Cynicism has become the standard for the evaluation of evidence, rather than being subject itself to evaluation by evidence. When the more educated are accused of saying only what they thought they ought to say thanks to their having had more education, actual evidence that such dissembling is going on is neither required nor produced, making the whole discussion futile. It is necessary only to assert that the better educated *might* be saying the socially desirable thing—not to prove that they are feigning a commitment to tolerance. In consequence, there has been no way to break out of this impasse in the conventional public opinion survey. It can always be objected that the more educated only appear more racially tolerant because they have learned what they are supposed to say, not because they mean what they say.

But by combining, through computer-assisted interviewing, the representational strengths of the standard public opinion survey with the power of experimental design, we have been able to break out of this impasse; and our findings have revealed two errors. On the one side, contemporary commentators on race have overestimated the extent to which racial double standards feed on particular political ideas, while on the other side underestimating the extent to which genuine evenhandedness is fostered through the process of education.

It is understandable that intellectuals, whose stock-in-trade is ideas, should attach importance to the role of ideas in public affairs, including the concepts of self-reliance and individual responsibility, not to mention conservatism as a political ideology, in promoting or legitimizing racial discrimination. But what renders people vulnerable to the practice of racial double standards is not that they have mastered and committed themselves to a particular body of ideas and thought. On the contrary, as the equal opportunity experiment showed, what most encourages the practice of racial double standards is precisely people's difficulty in understanding what the values they profess require of them; and education is bound up with acquiring the information and skills needed to think a political point of view through. Ideas may be dangerous, but an inability to understand them is even more so.

Moreover, the results of the equal opportunity experiment explode the notion that whites will say what they believe they are supposed to say about matters of race. Whites, it is commonly believed, will bias their answers in the course of an interview about politics to conceal their prejudice. They will thus make a show of supporting government assistance for blacks even though they actually oppose it; and they will do so in order to avoid conveying the impression that they are racist. There may indeed be a societal norm affecting white responses to blacks: some whites surely feel under pressure to say positive things about blacks, or at any rate not to say negative things. But *there is no societal norm that the government should do more to assist blacks.* The better educated people are, the more likely they are to treat the claims of blacks and whites to government assistance evenhandedly, not necessarily because they are more committed to racial equality, although it happens that they are. Rather, the crucial consideration in deciding their position on whether government should give blacks a particular form of government assistance is their overall outlook on politics—that is, whether they tend to be broadly liberal or conservative in outlook. They are, after all, being asked to take a position on a question of policy to which their ideological orientation is immediately relevant. If a person is liberal, and has a grip on what liberalism implies, then it is natural for him or her to suppose that the "right" answer to give is that government should assure equal opportunity to succeed; and support for governmental assurances of equal opportunity is the "right" answer from a liberal perspective whether the beneficiaries are blacks or women. Correspondingly, if a person is conservative, and has a grip on what conservatism entails, then it is natural for him or her to suppose that the "right" answer to give is that government should stay out of the business of equalizing opportunities; and a conservative will believe that this is exactly the answer expected of him or her whether the issue is framed in terms of blacks or of women. The better educated of both political stripes thus give equal treatment to the claims of blacks and women, not because they are acting out of a commitment to equal treatment as a value per se, but because they are acting in conformity with their ideological outlooks. Evenhandedness grows out of ideological consistency.

What has gone wrong in the understanding of race and politics is that politics has been omitted. Our sense of how Americans react to public policies dealing with blacks has been equated with how they feel about blacks. But disagreements over what government should, or should not, do in behalf of blacks are political, not private, disputes. And not the least reason it is necessary to distinguish public and private is that it is proper to disagree over political issues—indeed, perfectly legitimate to disagree if someone proposes that government step in and take care of a problem. There is a presumption in favor of government action from a liberal perspective; but there is a contrary presumption from a conservative one. The point is precisely that what *ought* to be done is exactly what is in dispute.

The failure to recognize how fully the politics of race is driven by political ideas has strengthened the supposition that it must be driven by more subterranean considerations. After all, commentators on all sides recognized the paradox: race prejudice—of the traditional variety—was in retreat; yet the discord over issues of race persisted and, in some ways, became even more divisive. So it seemed necessary to researchers of the 1970s and 80s to rethink what prejudice consists in, and how it fits into liberal democracy on the American model.

Racism, they came to insist, was now a prime expression of mainstream American values. It had wormed its way into the core of American society. Rather than being at odds with the Creed, racism was as American as apple pie. An array of ideas—that anybody can get ahead with hard work, that everyone ought to stand on his own two feet and take responsibility for his own life, that the person best qualified for a job should get it—ideas that once seemed to be homilies, are now said to be the wellsprings of contemporary racism.

The issue to focus on is not whether racism can sometimes find subtle expression—it manifestly can. Nor is it whether prejudice can opportunistically veil itself in support for social values or customs esteemed on other grounds—it surely can. Rather, the crucial issue is the claim that racial prejudice now has the out-and-out backing of America's most cherished values. Prejudice is not a product of what is most ignoble and self-serving in the American experience, as Gunnar Myrdal had suggested. Instead, in an irony which has escaped attention, during the very decades in which arguably the most ambitious and certainly the most costly attack on racism was ever mounted in American history, prejudice came to be seen as the product, in a telling phrase, of "the finest and proudest of American values."

There is a potential for irony here, albeit unintended. The notion that a man could pull himself up by his own efforts, that he was not a prisoner of his immediate circumstances, that he could achieve what he put his mind to, that he was not helplessly and inexorably confined to poverty had he the bad fortune to be born into it—all these ideas and their close companions brought alive, not only to many Americans born poor but to many more not even born American, that they could and should compete with anybody; that they were entitled to the same rights as anybody; that they were worth as much as anybody. Individualism, variously understood, has helped to provide the ideological underpinnings of American egalitarianism, and it is arresting to hear that individualism has become, in our time, the source of racism.

Ideas may change their character: because individualism once thrust in the direction of egalitarianism does not mean it will do so in every generation, and certainly opposition to a range of public policies to assist blacks (particularly by spending more money) has been accompanied by declarations that blacks should take more responsibility for dealing with their own problems. Yet strange as it may seem, for all the assertions that individualism and racism are now intimately tied together, no actual evidence of this has been put on the table. And as we have seen, the simple fact is that individualism has very little to do with racial attitudes. The indictment of the American ethos, leveled on the presumptive racism of individualism, rests on a confusion between individualistic values (individuality, competition, achievement, originality, and autonomy among them) and authoritarian values (order, obedience, authority, conformity, and power among them). It is the latter, not the former, that are tangled up in American racial attitudes both about blacks and about public policies dealing with blacks, a finding that teaches, among other lessons, that traditional values in a liberal society are not necessarily conservative—indeed, they can be liberal.

Racism is not built-in to the American ethos. Yet race manifestly persists as a central and divisive issue in American politics, and if the continuing clash over racial policy is not attributable to a new kind of racism, then to what is it attributable?

Prejudice is part of the politics of race, but a larger part is politics itself. And there, in politics, is where we find the greatest discontinuities between racial attitudes today and those that dominated a generation ago. The shape of racial politics in America has changed. Arguments over segregated schools and restrictive covenants and the poll tax were part of one overarching argument over whether blacks deserve to be treated as equals, with the position the public took on any given issue of race dictated in the largest measure by their feelings toward blacks. The battle against segregation (squabbles over issues like states' rights to one side) centered on the clash between two camps—one sympathetic to blacks, persuaded that they had been exploited and victimized, committed to the idea that they deserved equal treatment, and another camp, either indifferent to the plight of blacks or convinced of their inherent inferiority.

Today there *is* a politics to issues of race. Racial policies themselves—the specific goals they are intended to serve, and the particular means by which they propose to accomplish those goals—define significantly the structure of conflict over race. And, in consequence, the forces in play, the reasons why whites choose one or the other side of an issue of race, vary across racial issues and agendas.

Consider the role of ideology. The politics of the social welfare agenda bears the clear stamp of the classic argument in American politics between left and right. We do not mean of course that ideology drives the reactions of citizens *en bloc*. As a generation of public opinion research has made plain, overarching considerations of left and right are important chiefly to the more politically sophisticated and aware. But as we have seen, the dispute over issues such as whether government spending in behalf of blacks should be increased or blacks should take more responsibility for dealing with their own problems, particularly among the more aware and better educated part of the American public, is very much an extension of the long-running argument over government activism in behalf of the disadvantaged. It is a mistake, a deep and disfiguring mistake, to believe that racial politics does not take part in regular politics, to suppose that the clash of interests and ideas over issues of race is unique, independent of the differences that divide Americans over a range of issues.

Race prejudice *is* an ingredient of racial politics but in ways quite different from those commonly supposed. The conventional wisdom is that opposition to affirmative action is driven by racism, with the vehemence of whites' opposition to racial quotas and preferential treatment taken as proof of the tenacity of their prejudice against blacks. In fact, as we have seen, whites' feelings toward blacks are a minor factor in promoting opposition to affirmative action. Indeed, as the "mere mention" experiment demonstrated, apparent cause and effect can be reversed: dislike of affirmative action can engender dislike of blacks. In contrast to the race-conscious agenda where prejudice plays a minor role, in the social welfare agenda it is more central. The reactions of whites to racial issues on the social welfare agenda, our findings demonstrate, are powerfully shaped by their images of blacks as unwilling to make a genuine effort to deal with their own problems. Ironically, then, where racial stereotypes supposedly most inflame the thinking of whites about issues of race, their influence is weakest, and where their influence is least suspected, their impact is strongest.

At the deepest level, though, racial politics owes its shape not to beliefs or stereotypes distinctively about blacks but to the broader set of convictions about fairness and fair play that make up the American Creed. Although it never speaks with only one voice, the Creed has offered onesided support in favor of the principle of equal treatment; and policies that have as their objective seeing that blacks are treated the same as whites have the advantage of being consistent *with* the American Creed. In contrast, both proponents and opponents of social welfare policies can cite chapter and verse from the Creed legitimating their position—slightly different chapters and verses, to be sure, but equally legitimate ones all the same. Conflict over the social welfare agenda thus tends to reproduce a conflict *within* the Creed itself.

The race-conscious agenda offers yet a third variation on the relationship between race and the American Creed. Just because so many Americans are committed—imperfectly to be sure, but genuinely all the same—to the values of liberty and equality, they had no *principled* basis to object to the original civil rights movement; on the contrary, so far as the Creed was relevant, it pushed them to support equal treatment. Though there are elements of the Creed that can be deployed in favor of affirmative action, the fundamental ideas of fairness and equal treatment, for ordinary citizens, thrust in exactly the opposite direction. What gives the race-conscious agenda its distinctive character, what makes the agenda open to challenge morally, is that the principle of preferential treatment runs *against* the Creed.

Affirmative action—defined to mean preferential treatment—has become the chief item on the race-conscious agenda. It produces resentment and disaffection not because it assists blacks—substantial numbers of whites are prepared to support a range of policies to see blacks better off—but because it is judged to be unfair. Yet affirmative action is by no means the only factor encouraging racial discord. Protest over race has, perhaps inevitably but in any event tragically, been a victim of its success. A generation ago, the civil rights movement represented the moral high ground of American politics, dedicated to the values that blacks and whites share in common, and led by charismatic and courageous figures like Martin Luther King Jr. Almost immediately on the heels of its greatest successes, the Civil Rights Acts of 1964 and 1965, the voices of separatism began to drown out those of integration; and the headlines came to be dominated not by Martin Luther King Jr., but by Stokely Carmichael and H. Rap Brown, then, in the fullness of time, by Marion Barry, Tawana Brawley, and the Reverend Al Sharpton. Civil rights groups came to boycott not well-established businesses of white segregationists but tiny grocery stores run by Korean immigrants. Integration as a moral idea slipped away.

It cannot be said that the prime players in the politics of race—on any side—can claim credit for relieving racial rancor. Anger and resentment have become the common currency, as much among racial liberals as among racial conservatives. Ironically, the one-sided public focus of both on the race-conscious agenda and their comparative inattention to the agendas of social welfare and equal treatment have encouraged—subtly and unintentionally—the presumption that earlier, less ambitious, and ostensibly less controversial objectives have been substantially realized. It is thus taken for granted by many that we now find ourselves split over more ambitious policies for achieving racial equality, having worked our way through the "easy" part of the civil rights agenda focused on equal treatment. Yet the crux of the contemporary politics of race, as we have seen, consists precisely in the fact that, excepting only the issue of segregation in public institutions, all of the major issues of race—from government spending for blacks, through assurances of fair treatment in employment, to fair housing—are *still* on the table.

Of the myriad findings we have reported on contemporary American racial attitudes, the one to which we ourselves attach the most importance is the pliability of the policy positions of substantial numbers of whites on specific issues of race. It has long been assumed that whites are dug in on racial issues. In fact, large numbers of whites can be dislodged from the positions they have taken on many issues of race by calling their attention to countervailing considerations. And this underlines the quintessential feature of politics, including racial politics: majorities are not immutable facts of life permanently dictated by deep-lying social and economic forces. They are made—and unmade. A large enough number of Americans are open to argument to tip the scales, not on every issue of race but on the largest number of them. The case for public policies to assist blacks can be won; and it can be lost.

ABOUT THE SURVEYS

QUESTIONS FROM THE SURVEYS

QUESTIONNAIRE FOR THE RACE
AND POLITICS SURVEY

NOTES

BIBLIOGRAPHY

INDEX

ABOUT THE SURVEYS

RACE AND POLITICS SURVEY

The Race and Politics Survey was a random-digit telephone survey of English-speaking persons 18 years of age or older living in the five-county San Francisco-Oakland Bay Area. The survey included many experimental variations in question wording that were developed specifically for this study. Unless otherwise indicated, survey results presented in the book are based on this survey. The Survey Research Center of the University of California, Berkeley, conducted the survey from August through October 1986, using the CASES system for computer-assisted telephone interviewing. Interviews were completed with 1,113 persons, and the response rate was 68.1 percent. Results presented in this book are for non-Hispanic whites. Statistics are weighted to compensate for differences in probabilities of selection and for the number of adults and telephone lines in each selected household.

NATIONAL ELECTION STUDY

The National Election Study is an in-person interview conducted every two years by the Institute for Social Research at the University of Michigan. Each survey is an independently drawn sample of English-speaking persons 18 years of age or over, living in households within the United States. In 1986 2,176 persons were interviewed; a random half were administered

Form A, which contained most of the questions used in this book. Results presented are for non-Hispanic whites. Statistics are weighted by the number of eligible adults in the selected household.

GENERAL SOCIAL SURVEY

The General Social Survey is an in-person interview conducted every one or two years by the National Opinion Research Center in Chicago. Each survey is an independently drawn sample of English-speaking persons 18 years of age or over, living in households within the United States. In 1986 1,470 persons were interviewed. Results presented in this book are for non-Hispanic whites (those who did not say that their ancestors came from Mexico, Puerto Rico, or another Spanish-speaking country other than Spain). Statistics are weighted by the number of eligible adults in the selected household.

NATIONAL RACE SURVEY

The National Race Survey was a random-digit telephone survey of English-speaking persons 18 years of age or older living in the continental United States. The Survey Research Center of the University of California, Berkeley, conducted the survey from February through November 1991, using the CASES system for computer-assisted telephone interviewing. Interviews were completed with 2,223 persons, and the response rate was 65.3 percent. Results presented are comparisons between blacks and non-Hispanic whites. Statistics are weighted to compensate for differences in probabilities of selection and to balance the sample to 1990 Current Population Survey distributions of gender, race, age, and education.

KENTUCKY SURVEY

The Kentucky Survey was a small random-digit telephone survey of English-speaking whites 18 years of age or older living in the county containing the city of Lexington. The survey was carried out by the Survey Research Center of the University of Kentucky in October 1989. Interviews were completed with 253 persons.

QUESTIONS FROM THE SURVEYS

References are to the variable number in the NES codebook.

1. More government spending for blacks (var334)
   If you had a say in making up the federal budget this year, for which of the following programs would you like to see spending increased, and for which would you like to see spending decreased: (How about) programs that assist blacks?

2. Improve the socioeconomic position of blacks (var427)
   Some people feel that the government in Washington should make every effort to improve the social and economic position of blacks. Suppose these people are at one end of the scale at point number 1. Others feel that the government should not make any special effort to help blacks because they should help themselves. Suppose these people are at the other end, at point 7. And, of course, some other people have opinions somewhere in between at points 2, 3, 4, 5, or 6. Where would you place yourself on this scale, or haven't you thought much about this?

3. Affirmative action - jobs (var469)
   Some people say that because of past discrimination, blacks should be given preference in hiring and promotion. Others say that such preference

in hiring and promotion of blacks is wrong because it discriminates against whites. What about your opinion—are you for or against preferential hiring and promotion of blacks?

4. Affirmative action - college (var471)
Some people say that because of past discrimination it is sometimes necessary for colleges and universities to reserve openings for black students. Others oppose quotas because they say quotas discriminate against whites. What about your opinion—are you for or against quotas to admit black students?

GENERAL SOCIAL SURVEY

References are to the variable number and name in the GSS codebook.

1. More government spending for blacks (69F: natrace)
We are faced with many problems in this country, none of which can be solved easily or inexpensively. I'm going to name some of these problems, and for each one I'd like you to tell me whether you think we're spending too much money on it, too little money, or about the right amount: (How about) improving the condition of blacks?

2. Obligation to help (312: helpblk)
Some people think that blacks have been discriminated against for so long that the government has a special obligation to help improve their living standards. Others believe that the government should not be giving special treatment to blacks. Where would you place yourself on this scale, or haven't you made up your mind on this? [A card has a scale from 1 to 5, ranging from strongly agree the government is obligated to help blacks (1) to strongly agree that government shouldn't give special treatment (5).]

3. Busing (133: busing)
In general, do you favor or oppose the busing of black and white school children from one district to another?

4. Fair housing (127: racopen)
Suppose there is a community-wide vote on the general housing issue. There are two possible laws to vote on. One law says that a homeowner can decide for himself whom to sell his house to, even if he prefers not to sell to blacks. The second law says that a homeowner cannot refuse to sell to someone because of their race or color. Which law would you vote for?

5. Black president (135: racpres)
If your party nominated a black for President, would you vote for him if he were qualified for the job?

6. Integrate your child (132B: rachaf)
Would you yourself have any objection to sending your children to a school where half of the children are blacks?

NATIONAL RACE SURVEY

1. Stereotypes of blacks
Now I'll read a few words that people sometimes use to describe blacks. Of course, no word fits absolutely everybody, but as I read each one, please tell me using a number from 0 to 10 how well you think it describes blacks as a group. If you think it's a very good description of most blacks, give it a 10. If you feel a word is a very inaccurate description of most blacks, give it a 0.
How about:
  a. Aggressive or violent. (On a scale from 0 to 10, how well do you think it describes most blacks?)
  b. Lazy.
  c. Boastful.
  d. Irresponsible.
  e. Complaining.
[Nine positive stereotypes were also included in this series of questions.]

KENTUCKY SURVEY

1. Affirmative action—jobs
In a nearby state, an effort is being made to increase dramatically the number of blacks working in state government. This means that a large number of jobs will be reserved for blacks, even if their scores on merit exams are lower than those of whites who are turned down for the job. Do you favor or oppose this policy?

2. Stereotypes of blacks
Now I'm going to read a few statements that are sometimes used to describe blacks. Of course, no statement is true about everybody, but speaking generally please say whether you strongly agree, somewhat agree, somewhat disagree, or strongly disagree with each description. How about:
  a. Blacks have a tendency to be arrogant.
  b. Blacks tend to be family-oriented.
  c. (Blacks tend to be) lazy.
  d. Intelligent.
  e. Irresponsible.

f. Pleasure-loving.
g. Hard-working.
h. Friendly.
i. Violent.
j. Self-disciplined.

3. More government spending for blacks
Generally speaking, do you think the federal government is spending too much money, not enough money, or just about the right amount of money on programs that assist blacks?

QUESTIONNAIRE FOR THE RACE AND POLITICS SURVEY

This is a condensed version of the questionnaire used for computer-assisted telephone interviewing for the 1986 Race and Politics Survey. Administrative and computer-oriented material is excluded, but all of the substantive material is contained here.

Many questions in this interview had two or more randomized versions. Depending on the value of a random number generated for each such question for each respondent, the computer-assisted interviewing system would display the appropriate wording of the question to be read by the interviewer to the respondent. The values of the random numbers were then used to determine which version of a question each respondent answered.

INITIAL BACKGROUND QUESTIONS

1. First, we'd like to ask a few questions to make sure that we are talking to a genuinely representative cross section of the Bay Area community.

   How old were you on your last birthday?

2. In what state were you living around the time you were 16 years old?

3. What race or ethnic group do you consider yourself?
   [IF NECESSARY] We mean white, black, Asian, Mexican-American, Native American or what?

4. About how often do you attend religious services—every week, almost every week, once or twice a month, a few times a year or practically never?

5. What is your present religious preference—is it Protestant, Catholic, Jewish, or something else?

6. [CODE OR ASK IF NECESSARY] Is that a Christian or a non-Christian religion?

7. What religion were you raised in—was it Protestant, Catholic, Jewish, or something else?

PERSONAL VALUES

8. Next, some questions about what people consider important in life.

   How important is it to you to have a lot of money—very important, somewhat important, or not important to you?

9. How about following God's will—is THAT very important, somewhat important, or not important to you?

10. How important is it to you to compete against others to see how good you are?

11. How about preserving the traditional ideas of right and wrong?

12. How important is it to you to always be the best at what you do?

13. How about being accepted by other people, how important is that to you?

14. How important is it to you to do the things YOU want to do, even if it's not convenient for other people?

15. Now, thinking of the country as a whole, how important is it to maintain respect for America's power in the world, even if that means spending a lot of money on the military?

16. How important is it to encourage original ideas, even if it means less respect for authority?

17. Given the way things are these days, how important is it to strengthen law and order?

18. Now some community issues.

   [VERSION 1] Sometimes you hear it said that . . .

[VERSION 2] Many thoughtful people, after serious study and discussion, have come to the conclusion that...

... members of extreme political groups should NOT be allowed to hold public rallies in our cities. What about you—do you think members of extreme political groups should or should not be allowed to hold public rallies in our cities?

19. [VERSION 1] Many community organizations of parents and concerned citizens feel that . . .

[VERSION 2] Some people say that . . .

. . . books that preach the overthrow of the government should NOT be available in the public library. We'd like to know what you think. Do you think such books should or should not be available in the public library?

GOVERNMENT SPENDING

20. This country faces many problems, none of which can be solved easily or inexpensively. I'm going to name some of these problems. For each one, please tell me whether you think we're spending too much money on it, too little money, or about the right amount.

First, how about spending on the military, armaments, and defense—do you think we're spending too much money on that, too little money, or about the right amount?

21. How about spending on solving the problems of the big cities?

22. How about spending on halting the rising crime rate?

23. How about spending on welfare or public assistance for poor people?

WOMEN'S AND MEN'S ROLES

24. Here are some statements about the place of men and women in our society. For each statement, please say whether you agree strongly, agree somewhat, disagree somewhat, or disagree strongly.

When it comes to caring for babies and small children, men BY NATURE are less patient and giving than women.

25. There's something wrong with a woman who doesn't want to have children.

26. Without children, the average husband and wife wouldn't have very much to share or to talk about together.

27. Women don't get along with each other on the job as well as men do.

28. The only way that women will ever be paid the same as men for doing the same type of work is through constant protest and pressure.

GOVERNMENT HELP FOR THE UNEMPLOYED (VIGNETTES)

The next questions ask about people whose characteristics are varied at random according to the values of five random numbers. The five randomized characteristics are RACE (black or white), SEX (male or female), AGE (early twenties, mid-thirties, or early forties), MARITAL-PARENTAL STATUS (single, a single parent, married, or married and has children), and DEPENDABILITY (is or is not a dependable worker). Three such questions were asked, each time about a person with different randomized characteristics.

29. The next questions are about three different people who were laid off because the company where they worked had to reduce its staff. Think for a moment about each person and then tell me how much government help, if any, that person should receive while looking for a new job.

    The first [OR SECOND, OR THIRD] person is a [RACE] [SEX] in [HIS/HER] [AGE]. [HE/SHE] is [MARITAL-PARENTAL STATUS] and [DEPENDABILITY]. How much help in finding a new job do you think the government should give to this person—a lot, some, or none at all?

OPINIONS ABOUT LIFE IN AMERICA

30. The next statements are about life in America today. As I read each one, please tell me whether you basically agree or basically disagree.

    First: Too many people want someone else to help solve their problems instead of solving them themselves—do you basically agree or basically disagree with that statement?

    [IF MIXED FEELINGS] Even though you have mixed feelings, overall do you TEND to agree with it or to disagree with it?

31. Government officials usually pay more attention to a request or complaint from a black person than from other people.

    Do you basically agree or basically disagree with that statement?

32. While equal opportunity for . . .

    [VERSION 1] . . . blacks and minorities . . .

    [VERSION 2] . . . women . . .

    . . . to succeed is important, it's not really the government's job to guarantee it.

33. Respect for authority is one of the most important things that children should learn.

34. Most people who say that all races are equal really don't mean it.

35. Over the past few years, blacks have gotten less of the good things in life than they deserve.

36. Getting ahead in life depends on the advantages a person is born with rather than on a willingness to work hard.

37. Even though colleges admit blacks and other minority students these days, it doesn't mean that they're really giving minorities a chance to get a good education.

38. Research that might show minorities in a bad light . . .

    [VERSION 1] . . . should be banned because the results might strengthen racial stereotypes and prejudice.

    [VERSION 2] . . . should be banned.

39. People who fit most of their lives to a schedule probably miss most of the joy of living.

40. A good job is one where WHAT should be done and HOW it should be done are clearly defined.

41. Often the most interesting and stimulating people are those who don't mind being different and original.

42. The sooner we all acquire similar values and ideals, the better off we'll be.

SOCIAL POLICY ISSUES

43. Now some statements about issues in society today.

    Some people think that the government in Washington should increase spending for programs to help blacks. Others feel that blacks should rely only on themselves. Which makes more sense to you? Should the government help improve the position of blacks, or should they rely only on themselves?

[IF BOTH] If you had to choose, would you say government should help, or should blacks rely only on themselves?

[SKIPS:
   <1> Government should help   SKIP TO 44
   <2> Blacks should rely only on themselves SKIP TO 45]

44. Would you still feel that way even if government help means people get special treatment just because they are black or would that change your mind?

[SKIP TO 46].

45. Would you still feel that way even if it means that blacks will continue to be poorer and more often out of work than whites or would that change your mind?

46. Suppose there were a community-wide election on a general housing law and that you had to choose between two possible laws. One law says that homeowners can decide for themselves whom to sell their houses to, even if they prefer not to sell to blacks. The second law says that home-owners are not allowed to refuse to sell to someone because of race or color. Which law would you vote for—that homeowners can decide for themselves whom to sell to, or that homeowners can NOT refuse to sell to someone because of race or color?

[SKIPS:
   <1> Homeowners can decide for themselves SKIP TO 47
   <2> Homeowners canNOT refuse to sell   SKIP TO 48]

47. Would you feel differently if, as a result of that law, it turned out that blacks were prevented from moving into nice neighborhoods?

[SKIP TO 49]

48. Would you feel differently if it turned out that a new government agency had to be set up to enforce that law?

49. Some people feel that . . .

[VERSION 1] . . . the government in Washington . . .

[VERSION 2] . . . state or local government . . .

. . . ought to see to it that blacks get fair treatment in jobs. Others feel that this is not the government's business and it should stay out of it.

How do you feel, should . . .

[VERSION 1] . . . the government in Washington . . .

[VERSION 2] . . . state or local government . . .

. . . see to it that blacks get fair treatment in jobs or should it stay out of it?

[SKIPS:
  <1> government should see
      that blacks get fair treatment   SKIP TO 50
  <2> government should stay out of it   SKIP TO 51]

50. Would you still feel the same way, even if it means that government will have more say in telling people how to run their lives, or do you think that might change your mind?

[SKIP TO 52]

51. Would you still feel the same way even if it means that some racial discrimination will continue?

52. [VERSION 1] The Congress of the United States—both the House of Representatives and the Senate—have passed laws . . .

[VERSION 2] Sometimes you hear it said that there should be a law . . .

. . . to ensure that a certain number of federal contracts go to minority contractors. We'd like to know what YOU think. Do you think that such a law is a good idea or a bad idea?

53. Do you feel strongly or not so strongly about this?

54. Some people say that because of past discrimination it is sometimes necessary for colleges and universities to reserve openings for black students who don't meet the usual standards. Others are against such quotas. What's your opinion—are you for or against quotas to admit some black students who don't meet the usual standards?

[SKIPS:
  <1> favor quotas   SKIP TO 55
  <2> oppose quotas   SKIP TO 56]

55. Would you still feel that way, even if it means fewer opportunities for qualified whites, or would you change your mind?

[SKIP TO 57]

56. Would you still feel that way, even if it means that hardly any blacks

would be able to go to the best colleges and universities, or would you change your mind?

57. Some people think achieving racial integration of schools is so important that it justifies busing children to schools out of their own neighborhoods. Others think letting children go to their neighborhood schools is so important that they oppose busing. How about you—do you favor or oppose busing?

EXPLANATIONS FOR RACIAL INEQUALITY

[IF R IS BLACK, SKIP TO 67]

58. Most people—blacks and whites alike—agree that the average white person in America is more likely to have a good income, get a good education, and to have a regular job than the average black is. Here are some of the reasons that have been given as to why the average black American is not as well off as the average white American. As I read each one, please tell me whether you basically agree or disagree.

First, how about the statement that rich and powerful white people who control things in America try to keep black people down—do you basically agree or basically disagree with that explanation as to why the average black American is not as well off as the average white American?

59. How about the statement that God made the races different as part of his divine plan?

60. If blacks would only try harder, they would be just as well off as whites.

61. A history of slavery and being discriminated against has created conditions that make it difficult for black people to work their way up.

62. The reason most black people are not as well off as most whites is that blacks are born with less ability.

PREJUDICIAL STEREOTYPES OF BLACKS

[IF R IS BLACK, SKIP TO 67]

63. Now I'm going to read a few more statements about black people. No statement is true about everybody, but, speaking generally, please say whether you agree strongly, agree somewhat, disagree somewhat, or disagree strongly with each statement.

How about the statement: Most blacks have a chip on their shoulder.

64. Blacks are more violent than whites.

65. Black neighborhoods tend to be run down because blacks simply don't take care of their property.

66. Most blacks who are on welfare programs could get a job if they really tried.

ATTITUDES TOWARD JEWS

[IF R's RELIGION OR RACE IS JEWISH, SKIP TO 71]

67. Now, I'm going to read you some statements about Jews. Once again, no statement is true of all people, but please tell me, speaking generally, whether you agree or disagree with the statement.

First: Jews are more willing than others to use shady practices to get ahead. Would you say that you agree strongly, agree somewhat, disagree somewhat, or disagree strongly with that statement?

68. How about: Most Jews try to support community institutions like the public school system.

69. Most Jews don't care what happens to people who aren't Jewish.

70. Most Jews are pushy.

CONCEPT OF PREJUDICE

71. We're almost finished now. But I have just a few questions about prejudice. While most Americans feel that prejudice is wrong, there's a lot of disagreement about what prejudice really MEANS. We'd like to try and find out what people in the Bay Area see as prejudice.

Suppose someone says that blacks tend to be more hostile than whites. Would you say making that statement probably IS, or probably IS NOT, a sign of prejudice?

72. Suppose someone says that the average white person is more intelligent than the average black person.

73. Suppose someone says that blacks tend to have a chip on their shoulder.

CHRISTIAN PARTICULARISM

[IF R DID NOT DESCRIBE HIS/HER CURRENT RELIGION AS CHRISTIAN, THEN SKIP TO 75]

74. On another topic, how necessary for salvation is belief in Jesus Christ—

would you say that it is absolutely necessary for salvation, it probably would help in gaining salvation, or that it probably has no influence on salvation?

[IF R ASKS FOR DEFINITION] Salvation means being saved so you can go to heaven.

POLITICAL PARTY AND IDEOLOGY

75. Before we finish the interview, we would like to get a little more background information for statistical purposes.

Generally speaking, do you usually think of yourself as a REPUBLICAN, a DEMOCRAT, an INDEPENDENT, or what?

[SKIPS:
   <1> Republican   SKIP TO 76
   <3> Democrat   SKIP TO 77
   <5> Independent

   <6> No preference
   <7> Other (SPECIFY)

SKIP TO 78]

76. Would you call youself a STRONG Republican or a NOT VERY STRONG Republican?

[SKIP TO 79]

77. Would you call yourself a STRONG Democrat or a NOT VERY STRONG Democrat?

[SKIP TO 79]

78. Do you think of yourself as closer to the Republican Party or to the Democratic Party?

79. In general, when it comes to politics, do you usually think of yourself as a liberal, a conservative, a moderate, or what?

[SKIPS:
   <1> Liberal   SKIP TO 80
   <3> Conservative SKIP TO 81
   <5> Moderate   SKIP TO 82

   <7> Never think of myself in those terms

   <8> Don't know (after probe for opinion)

SKIP TO 83]

80. Do you think of yourself as a strong liberal or a not very strong liberal?

[SKIP TO 83]

81. Do you think of yourself as a strong conservative or a not very strong conservative?

[SKIP TO 83]

82. Do you think of yourself as more like a liberal or more like a conservative?

FINAL BACKGROUND QUESTIONS

83. CODE OR ASK IF NECESSARY: What sex are you?

84. What is the highest grade of school or year of college you COMPLETED?

85. Are you now married, or are you living with someone in a marriage-like relationship, widowed, divorced, separated, or have you never been married?

[IF R IS NOT MARRIED, SKIP TO 87]

86. What is the highest grade of school or year of college your SPOUSE completed?

87. We'd like to know if you are now employed full-time, employed part-time, on temporary layoff, unemployed and looking for work, retired, a student, (a housewife), or what?

[IF R ASKS] By full time, we mean 35 or more hours per week.

88. [CODE OR ASK IF NECESSARY]

Have you ever had a job for pay?

[IF NOT, SKIP TO 91]

89. What (is/was) your main occupation? What sort of work (do/did) you do?

[IF R NOT CURRENTLY EMPLOYED, ASK ABOUT MOST RECENT JOB FOR PAY]

90. (Do/Did) you belong to a labor union?

[IF R IS NOT MARRIED, SKIP TO 95]

91. We'd like to know if your SPOUSE is now employed full-time, em-

ployed part-time, or is he/she on temporary lay-off, unemployed and look-ing for work, retired, a student, (a housewife), or what?

92. [CODE OR ASK IF NECESSARY]

    Has he/she ever had a job for pay?

93. What [is/was] [his/her] main occupation? What sort of work [does/did] [he/she] do?

94. [Does/Did] your SPOUSE belong to a labor union?

95. How long have you lived in your present house or apartment?

    [INTERVIEWER: ROUND TO YEARS]

96. Are there any children living in your household who go to public grade school or high school or who will be starting public school in the next few months?

97. Are there any children under the age of six living in your household?

98. How many telephones, counting extensions, do you have in your home?

    [IF ONLY ONE, SKIP TO 101]

99. Do (both/all) the telephones have the same number?

    [IF YES, SKIP TO 101]

100. How many different numbers are there?

101. We're interested in how people are getting along financially these days. Would you say that you (and members of your family living with you) are better off or worse off financially than you were a year ago?

102. Think of the income BEFORE taxes of ALL MEMBERS of your household living with you in 1985, and include as income: pensions, dividends, interest, and all other income. What was the total income from all sources (including your own) in 1985 BEFORE TAXES?

    [A series of questions was asked, to determine whether income was above or below certain amounts.]

    Those are all the questions I have. Thank you very much, we really appreciate your help and the time you've given us. Goodbye.

NOTES

INTRODUCTION

2 "The American Negro problem": Gunnar Myrdal, *An American Dilemma* (1944), p. xlvii.
3 "which refer to man as such": Myrdal, p. xlviii.
— "worships the Constitution": Myrdal, p. 14.
— "the whole issue": Myrdal, p. 383.
— "the true hypocrit": Myrdal, p. 21.

1. THE VARIETY OF RACIAL POLITICS

16 "easy issue": See Edward G. Carmines and James A. Stimson, *Issue Evolution* (1989); their pioneering study was the first to work through systematically the idea that race represents not merely a social but distinctively a political problem.
18 "to boil down to the same single question": Philip E. Converse, "The nature of belief systems in mass publics" (1964), p. 235.
19 "Carmines and Stimson": The numbers are taken from Edward G. Carmines and James Stimson, *Issue Evolution* (1989), p. 122; the original analysis was performed by Norman H. Nie, Sidney Verba, and John R. Petrocik, *The Changing American Voter* (1976). The coefficient used then was gamma; we shall use for our analyses the Pearson

product moment correlation coefficient, because it gives more conservative estimates.

32 "there should be separate sections": Howard Schuman, Charlotte Steeh, and Lawrence Bobo, in *Racial Attitudes in America* (1985), provide the best source for trend data on American attitudes toward the problem of race at the level of both principle and policy.

2. PICTURES IN THE MIND

38 "apparent anomaly": Jennifer Hochschild, *The New American Dilemma: Liberal Democracy and School Desegregation* (1984), p. 5.

39 "Crosby and her colleagues": Faye Crosby, S. Bromley, and L. Saxe, "Recent unobtrusive studies of black and white discrimination and prejudice: a literature review" (1980).

44 "Andrew Hacker": All of these numbers are from Andrew Hacker, *Two Nations* (1992), which provides a wealth of figures on the contemporary condition of blacks.

46 "a substantial and distinguished body of research": Samuel Stouffer, *Communism, Conformity, and Civil Liberties* (1955). The basic argument was subsequently developed, under Charles Y. Glock, into the most comprehensive, quantitative study of prejudice (of various forms) in America. Among the research program's principal publications are Gertrude Selznick and Stephen Steinberg, *The Tenacity of Prejudice* (1969); Richard A. Apostle, Charles Y. Glock, Thomas Piazza, and Marijean Suelzle, *The Anatomy of Racial Attitudes* (1983); and Harold E. Quinley and Charles Y. Glock, *Anti-Semitism in America* (1979).

52 "the technical name": Quoted by Roger Brown, *Social Psychology* (1986), p. 533.

53 "Charles Y. Glock": See Gertrude Selznick and Stephen Steinberg, *The Tenacity of Prejudice* (1969), and Harold E. Quinley and Charles Y. Glock, *Anti-Semitism in America* (1979).

57 "hard work, individualism": John McConahay and Joseph C. Hough, Jr., "Symbolic racism" (1976), p. 40.

58 "Louis Hartz": Louis Hartz, *The Liberal Tradition in America* (1955).
— "a form of resistance": Donald R. Kinder and David O. Sears, "Prejudice and politics" (1981), p. 416.

3. COVERT RACISM AND DOUBLE STANDARDS

68 "violate cherished values": John B. McConahay, "Modern racism, ambivalence, and the modern racism scale" (1986).

74 "social responsibility": Herbert Hyman, "Social psychology and race relations" (1969).

4. PREJUDICE AND POLITICS

89 "following standard practice": The canonical definition of prejudice is supplied by John Harding, Bernard Kutner, Harold Proshansky, and Isidor Chein, "Prejudice and ethnic relations" (1954).

5. THREE AGENDAS

113 "as Hacker reports": Andrew Hacker, *Two Nations* (1992).
121 "conjunction": Donald R. Kinder and David O. Sears, "Prejudice and politics" (1981).
130 "1988 Harris Poll": Harris Poll, *Business Week*, March 14, 1988 pp. 65–68.

6. CHANGING MINDS ABOUT RACE

153 "Philip Converse": Philip E. Converse, "Attitudes and non-attitudes: Continuation of a dialogue" (1970).
157 "limited to one class": Carl I. Hovland and Irving L. Janis, "An overview of persuasibility research" (1959).

CONCLUSION: IRONIES

174 "the finest and proudest": David O. Sears, "Symbolic racism" (1988).

BIBLIOGRAPHY

Adorno, Theodor, Else Frenkel-Brunswik, Daniel Levinson, and R. Nevitt Sanford. 1950. *The Authoritarian Personality*. New York: Harper.

Altemeyer, Bob. 1988. *Enemies of Freedom: Understanding Right Wing Authoritarianism*. San Francisco: Jossey-Bass.

Apostle, Richard A., Charles Y. Glock, Thomas Piazza, and Marijean Suelzle. 1983. *The Anatomy of Racial Attitudes*. Berkeley: University of California Press.

Bellah, Robert N., Richard Madsen, William M. Sullivan, Ann Swidler, and Steven M. Tipton. 1985. *Habits of the Heart: Individualism and Commitment in American Life*. Berkeley: University of California Press.

Black, Earl, and Merle Black. 1987. *Politics and Society in the South*. Cambridge: Harvard University Press.

Brown, Peter. 1991. *Minority Party: Why Democrats Face Defeat in 1992 and Beyond*. Washington, D.C.: Regnery Gateway.

Brown, Roger W. 1986. *Social Psychology*. 2d ed. New York: Free Press.

Carmines, Edward G., and James A. Stimson. 1989. *Issue Evolution: Race and the Transformation of American Politics*. Princeton: Princeton University Press.

Christie, Richard, and Marie Jahoda, eds. 1954. *Studies in the Scope and Method of "The Authoritarian Personality."* Glencoe, Ill.: Free Press.

Converse, Philip E. 1964. "The nature of belief systems in mass publics." In David E. Apter, ed., *Ideology and Discontent*, pp. 206–261. New York: Free Press.

——— 1970. "Attitudes and non-attitudes: Continuation of a dialogue." In Edward R. Tufte, ed., *The Quantitative Analysis of Social Problems*, pp. 168–189. Reading, Mass.: Addison-Wesley.

Crosby, Faye, Stephanie Bromley, and Leonard Saxe. 1980. "Recent unobtrusive studies of black and white discrimination and prejudice: A literature review." *Psychological Bulletin* 87:546–563.

Delli Carpini, Michael X., and Scott Keeter. 1991. "Stability and change in the U.S. public's knowledge of politics." *Public Opinion Quarterly* 55:583–612.

Dionne, E. J. 1991. *Why Americans Hate Politics*. New York: Simon and Schuster.

Dovidio, John F., and Samuel L. Gaertner, eds. 1986. *Prejudice, Discrimination and Racism*. New York: Academic Press.

Edsall, Thomas Byrne, and Mary D. Edsall. 1991. *Chain Reaction: The Impact of Race, Rights, and Taxes on American Politics*. New York: Norton.

Fletcher, Joseph F., and Marie-Christine Chalmers. 1991. "Attitudes of Canadians toward affirmative action: Opposition, value pluralism and nonattitudes." *Political Behavior* 13:67–95.

Greeley, Andrew M., and Paul B. Sheatsley. 1971. "Attitudes toward racial integration." *Scientific American* 225:13–19.

Groves, Robert M., and Robert L. Kahn. 1979. *Surveys by Telephone*. New York: Academic Press.

Hacker, Andrew. 1992. *Two Nations: Black and White, Separate, Hostile, Unequal*. New York: Charles Scribners Sons.

Harding, John, Bernard Kutner, Harold Proshansky, and Isidor Chein. 1954. "Prejudice and ethnic relations." In Gardner Lindzey, ed., *Handbook of Social Psychology*, 1st ed., pp. 1021–1061. Reading, Mass.: Addison-Wesley.

Harris Poll, *Business Week*, March 14, 1988, pp. 65–68.

Hartz, Louis. 1955. *The Liberal Tradition in America*. New York: Harcourt Brace.

Hochschild, Jennifer. 1981. *What's Fair? American Beliefs about Distributive Justice*. Cambridge: Harvard University Press.

——— 1984. *The New American Dilemma: Liberal Democracy and School Desegregation*. New Haven: Yale University Press.

Hovland, Carl I., and Irving L. Janis. 1959. "An overview of persuasibility research." In Carl I. Hovland and Irving L. Janis, eds., *Personality and Persuasibility*, pp. 11–28. New Haven: Yale University Press.

Hyman, Herbert H. 1969. "Social psychology and race relations." In Irwin Katz and Patricia Gurin, eds., *Race and the Social Sciences*, pp. 3-48. New York: Basic Books.

Hyman, Herbert H., and Paul B. Sheatsley. 1956. "Attitudes toward desegregation." *Scientific American* 195:35–39.

———— 1964. "Attitudes toward desegregation." *Scientific American* 211:16–23.

Hyman, Herbert H., Charles R. Wright, and John Shelton Reed. 1975. *The Enduring Effects of Education.* Chicago: University of Chicago Press.

Jackman, Mary R. 1978. "General and applied tolerance: Does education increase commitment to racial integration?" *American Journal of Political Science* 22:302–324.

———— 1981. "Education and policy commitment to racial integration." *American Journal of Political Science* 25:256–269.

Jackman, Robert W. 1972. "Political elites, mass publics, and support for democratic principles." *Journal of Politics* 48(2):256–269.

Jackson, Walter A. 1990. *Gunnar Myrdal and America's Conscience: Social Engineering and Racial Liberation 1938–1987.* Chapel Hill: University of North Carolina Press.

Jaynes, Gerald David, and Robin M. Williams, Jr. 1989. *A Common Destiny: Blacks and American Society.* Washington, D.C.: National Academy of Science Press.

Kinder, Donald R. 1986. "The continuing American dilemma: White resistance to racial change 40 years after Myrdal." *Journal of Social Issues* 42:151–172.

Kinder, Donald R., and David O. Sears. 1981. "Prejudice and politics: Symbolic racism versus racial threats to the good life." *Journal of Personality and Social Psychology* 40:414–431.

Lasch, Christopher. 1991. *The True and Only Heaven: Progress and Its Critics.* New York: Norton.

Lipmann, Walter. 1922. *Public Opinion.* New York: Harcourt Brace.

Lipset, Seymour Martin, and William Schneider. 1978. "The Bakke Case: How would it be decided at the bar of public opinion?" *Public Opinion,* March–April, pp. 38–44.

McClosky, Herbert, and John Zaller. 1984. *The American Ethos: Public Attitudes toward Capitalism and Democracy.* Cambridge: Cambridge University Press.

McConahay, John B. 1986. "Modern racism, ambivalence, and the Modern Racism Scale." In John F. Dovidio and Samuel L. Gaertner, eds., *Prejudice, Discrimination and Racism: Theory and Research.* New York: Academic Press.

McConahay, John B., Betty B. Hardee, and Valerie Batts. 1981. "Has racism declined in America? It depends on who is asking and what is asked." *Journal of Conflict Resolution* 25:23-39.

McConahay, John B., and Joseph C. Hough, Jr. 1976. "Symbolic racism." *Journal of Social Issues* 32:23–39.

McGuire, William. 1985. "The nature of attitudes and attitude change." In Gardner Lindzey and Elliot Aronson, eds., *Handbook of Social Psychology,* 3d ed., pp. 233–346. Reading, Mass.: Addison-Wesley.

Myrdal, Gunnar. 1944. *An American Dilemma.* New York: Harper and Row.

Nie, Norman H., Sidney Verba, and John R. Petrocik. 1979. *The Changing American Voter.* Cambridge: Harvard University Press.

Pettigrew, Thomas. 1979. "Racial change and social policy." *Annals of the American Academy of Political and Social Science* 44:114–131.

Piazza, Thomas, Paul M. Sniderman, and Philip E. Tetlock. 1990. "Analysis of the dynamics of political reasoning: A general-purpose computer-assisted methodology." In James Stimson, ed., *Political Analysis, Vol. 1.* Ann Arbor: University of Michigan Press.

Quinley, Harold E., and Charles Y. Glock. 1979. *Anti-Semitism in America.* New York: Free Press.

Rossi, Peter H., and Steven L. Nock, eds. 1982. *Measuring Social Judgments: The Factorial Survey Approach.* Beverly Hills: Sage.

Schuman, Howard, and Lawrence Bobo. 1988. "Survey-based experiments on white racial attitudes toward residential integration." *American Journal of Sociology* 94(2):273–299.

Schuman, Howard, and Stanley Presser. 1981. *Questions and Answers.* New York: Academic Press.

Schuman, Howard, Charlotte Steeh, and Lawrence Bobo. 1985. *Racial Attitudes in America.* Cambridge: Harvard University Press.

Sears, David O. 1983. "The persistence of early political predispositions." In Ladd Wheeler and Philip Shaver, eds., *Review of Personality and Social Psychology.* Beverly Hills: Sage.

———— 1988. "Symbolic racism." In Phyllis A. Katz and Dalmas A. Taylor, eds., *Eliminating Racism.* New York: Plenum Press.

Sears, David O., and Jack Citrin. 1985. *Tax Revolt: Something for Nothing in California.* Cambridge: Harvard University Press.

Sears, David O., Carl P. Hensler, and Leslie K. Speer. 1979. "Whites' opposition to 'busing': Self-interest or symbolic politics?" *American Political Science Review* 73:369–384.

Sears, David O., and Donald R. Kinder. 1971. "Racial tensions and voting in Los Angeles." In W. Z. Hirsch, ed., *Los Angeles: Viability and Prospects for Metropolitan Leadership.* New York: Praeger.

Selznick, Gertrude, and Stephen Steinberg. 1969. *The Tenacity of Prejudice.* New York: Harper and Row.

Sleeper, Jim. 1991. *The Closest of Strangers: Liberalism and the Politics of Race in New York.* New York: Norton.

Sniderman, Paul M., Richard A. Brody, and Philip E. Tetlock. 1991. *Reasoning and Choice: Explorations in Political Psychology.* New York: Cambridge University Press.

Sniderman, Paul M., Thomas Piazza, Philip E. Tetlock, and Ann Kendrick. 1991. "The new racism." *American Journal of Political Science* 35(2):423–447.

Sniderman, Paul M., and Philip E. Tetlock. 1986a. "Symbolic racism: Problems of motive attribution in political analysis." *Journal of Social Issues* 42:129–150.

———— 1986b. "Reflections on American racism." *Journal of Social Issues* 42:173–187.

Southern, David W. 1987. *Gunnar Myrdal and Black-White Relations: The Use and Abuse of* An American Dilemma, *1944–1969*. Baton Rouge: Louisiana State University Press.

Stouffer, Samuel. 1955. *Communism, Conformity and Civil Liberties*. New York: Doubleday.

Taylor, D. Garth, Paul B. Sheatsley, and Andrew M. Greeley. 1978. "Attitudes toward racial integration." *Scientific American* 238:42–51.

Taylor-Booby, Peter. 1991. "Ideology, attitudes and the future of welfare citizenship: Welfare state regimes and women's unwaged work." Paper presented at the conference on The Quality of Citizenship, Department of General Social Sciences, University of Utrecht, March 20–22.

Terkel, Studs. 1992. *Race: How Blacks and Whites Think and Feel about the American Obsession*. New York: New Press.

Wilson, William Julius. 1987. *The Truly Disadvantaged: The Inner City, the Underclass, and Public Policy*. Chicago: University of Chicago Press.

INDEX

Race (general discussion): patterns of conflict over, 5–6, 26–28; revisionist view of, 120–121. *See also* Issues of race; Politics of race; Racial policies; Racism

Race and Politics (RAP) Survey, 20, 25–28, 41, 45, 50, 114, 130, 142, 181; questionnaire, 187–198

Race-conscious agenda, 8–9, 13, 21, 22, 32, 34, 97–101, 103, 109, 112, 115, 128–134, 140, 145, 176, 177, 178

Racism, 5–7; covert/subtle, 2, 36, 39, 65, 66, 68–69, 86–87, 172, 174; traditional American values and, 2–4, 12, 37–38, 57, 63, 68–69, 84–86, 173–175, 176–177; overt, 6, 12, 44–45, 64, 167; source of, 81. *See also* "New racism"

Sanford, Nevitt, 52
Segregation, 139, 175, 178; laws, 33
Selznick, Gertrude, 53
Separatism, black, 129, 177
Set-asides, 20, 32, 131–133
Sharpton, Al, 177
Slavery, 41, 80, 114, 115
Social welfare agenda, 2, 8–9, 21, 22, 26, 31, 32, 34, 112–121, 128, 145; prejudice and, 92–97, 107, 120, 176, 178; white public opinion on, 103, 118, 140, 141–146; politics of, 110–113, 121, 122, 129, 135, 148, 164–165, 175–176; ideology and, 116–117, 119–120, 121, 122, 154–155, 160–162, 172–173, 175–176; pliability of opinion on, 145, 146, 147–148, 150, 164–165. *See also* Affirmative action; Fair housing
Stereotypes, racial, 5, 36–37, 126, 167–168; prejudice and, 8, 43, 51–56, 89, 105; unprejudiced people and, 8, 97; overt expression of, 12, 44–45, 64;

response to government assistance and, 34, 69–78, 90, 92–93, 98; response to racial policies and, 34, 104–109, 176; traditional American values and, 35, 37–38, 58–61, 69, 70; covert endorsement of, 36; psychology of, 37, 51–56; sources of, 37; negative characterizations of blacks by whites, 38–46, 51, 91, 108, 168; elements of truth in, 44, 46, 89; negative characterizations of blacks by blacks, 44–46, 108; acceptance of, 46–51, 55, 68, 89, 94, 103; effect of education on, 50, 64–65; ethnocentrism and, 52–53; "new" racism and, 56–63, 64–65; ideology and, 79, 81; issues of race and, 88–89, 91; systematic endorsement of, 89–92; Overall Index of, 92–93; political effects of, 94–95, 105–106, 109; effect of geographic location on, 95
Stereotypes, religious (anti-Semitism), 7, 37, 53–55, 57, 92, 105, 107, 118, 125, 126, 167–168
Sumner, William Graham, 52

Tolerance, 30, 48, 87, 125; effect of education on, 13, 46–47, 55, 81–82, 83, 87, 170, 171

Unemployment rates, 113

Values, traditional American, 3–4, 57–58, 129–130; racism and, 2–4, 12, 37–38, 57, 63, 68–69, 84–86, 173–175, 176–177; authoritarian, 6, 12, 59, 61–63, 65, 175; individualistic, 6, 65, 174, 175; racial stereotypes and, 35, 37–38, 58–61, 69, 70; education and, 46–47; Protestant ethic, 57; ideology and, 58; double standards and, 84–86; prejudice and, 174; racial policies and, 176–177